The Mouseketeer That Roared

Eileen Rogosin

Theme Park Press
The Happiest Books on Earth
www.ThemeParkPress.com

Editor: Bob McLain
Layout: Artisanal Text

ISBN 978-1-68390-258-4
Printed in the United States of America

Theme Park Press | www.ThemeParkPress.com
Address queries to bob@themeparkpress.com

This book is dedicated to my mother,
Hannah Thurschwell Diamond

Dear Mom,

How long has it been now? We haven't communicated in such a long time. We're both so far removed from one another. My thoughts are of you. Are you well? Are they taking good care of you? Do you remember me? Look where we are now—worlds apart. Not only in distance. I am just beginning to learn to live.

Did I ever thank you for giving me everything you had in your power to give? For mothering me, loving me, caring for me and encouraging me to go on because you believed in me.

I'm letting go for the first time: And learning to believe in myself.

Separation, I suppose, is normal between a child and a parent. Mine came late, but it has come. I want you to know I'm okay, Mom. You put me on a good path. Even though I'm still putting on the finishing touches. I like me.

I still need you— Mother me again. I'm not as strong as I say. It's nice to know I can still turn to you—or can I? Listen: time is passing. You're gone now. I miss you. Please don't go yet. Not yet.

I love you Mom.

Good-bye.

Contents

Foreword

Like so many in grammar school during the 50s, I always ran home from school to see Walt Disney's Mouseketeers, lamenting that I wasn't one of those lucky kids. I remember one show in particular, where a pretty but pretentious girl in a frilly gown, played Beethoven's "Für Elise" which I was studying at the time. All I could think of was that she was pretty but I played better, which may or may not have been true. But clearly, I was competitive from that early age.

Imagine my shock to find out the girl I fell in love with while a student at UCLA was the same pretentious pianist from the Mouseketeers. Her name was, and still is, Eileen.

—Roy Rogosin

Mickey Mouse Club, December 31, 1956

Introduction

I've been writing on *The Mouseketeer That Roared* over the years to remember my life experiences and help those young people who are just beginning their paths into the performing arts. I was so lucky at an early age to discover what I loved to do.

I remember when I was a little girl in my back yard in Hollywood on Beachwood Drive, gathering all my relatives and friends for an impromptu performance on my tricycle, singing, "Zipadee DooDah, Zipadee Aay," I put a beautiful blue damask tablecloth on the ground to be my stage and drove on it singing, "My, oh my what a wonderful day." Disney had already entered my life as soon as I saw *The Song of the South*. And then, to finish with a bang, I got off my tricycle, stretched my arms over my head, announced that I was five years old, and turned and turned like a ballerina, before making a dramatic bow in front of my adoring audience. My mom was horrified when I finished and she saw the tire tracks on her beloved heirloom. I knew from that moment that I was destined to be a great singer and dancer.

So, this book is a promise to all young performers that, if you have a dream, and are disciplined and faithful in pursuing it, you will succeed.

CHAPTER ONE

City of Angels and Tinsel

Hi, and welcome to my life!

I was born in Hollywood, California in 1943 and started working professionally at age 6. Had I been born in Minnesota or Montana, things would have turned out very differently, and you would probably not be reading this memoir, nor would I have written it.

When I started doing my research on early Hollywood, I was surprised to learn that it was a rural community in 1870 consisting of ranches, orchards and farms. It was incorporated as a municipality in 1903 and merged with the city of Los Angeles in 1910.

Shortly thereafter, a prominent film industry emerged, and by 1920 Hollywood films were the fifth largest private industry in the nation.

The Charlie Chaplin Studios opened in 1917, quickly followed by Columbia Pictures, RKO, MGM, Warner Brothers, Universal Studios, Paramount and Disney Studios. Little did I know that I was to become an integral part of the house that Mickey built!

Hollywood was my hometown. I grew up in a Craftsman bungalow on Beachwood Drive, underneath the Hollywood sign. I remember the building of the Hollywood Freeway in 1951. Mountains were torn down and trolley-car tracks were removed from Hollywood Boulevard.

When I started preparing to write about my background and career, I was curious about what was happening in Hollywood in 1943, when I was born.

The Diamond Family: L-R Harriet, Hannah, Harry & Eileen, mid-1940s.

I discovered that it was already a rich and fertile creative community.

1943 Hollywood Cavalcade Newsreels filmed and broadcast daily World War II news from many small shops along Hollywood Boulevard.

The Stage Door Canteen featured big stars entertaining the troops.

The now-classic film *Casablanca* was the subtlest of all wartime propaganda films, animated by the irresistible love story between Humphrey Bogart and Ingrid Bergman. "Here's looking at you, kid" became part of the vernacular of the day and the song, "As Time Goes By" is still recognized as one of the truly great film songs. *Casablanca* won the Oscar for best motion picture.

The 16th Annual Academy Awards were held at Grauman's Chinese Theater, and free passes were given out to men and women in uniform. Jack Benny was master of ceremonies for the event, which lasted less than thirty minutes!

CHAPTER TWO
Look, Ma, I'm Dancing!

My mother was, by far, my biggest fan and greatest supporter from the very start. She encouraged me to start dance and piano lessons. She drove me all over Hollywood so that I could attend the best dancing schools with the best teachers, many of whom were stars in their own right. I didn't really know at the time that she was living her dream through me, as so many other stage mothers. But, unlike some other mother-daughter show business sagas, our relationship was positive and always mutually rewarding. It was fun for both of us, and that sense of fun has stayed with me throughout my career.

Age 11.

All of my teachers were working professionals. They performed in world-famous ballet companies, danced on movie sets, and shared their passions with their students.

Rainbow Studios, a rehearsal space with dance classrooms, was where my love affair with dance began. It was there that I experienced world-class teachers who were devoted to inspiring young and impressionable dancers like me!

One of my most unforgettable and cherished memories was with my first ballet teacher, Michael Panaieff. He lifted me onto his shoulders and carried me across the room, repeating the whole time, "YOU ARE A BALLERINA!" "BE A BALLERINA!" At that moment, I soared...weightless, arms extended, head back...reaching for the stars.

Mel Dangcil was our classroom pianist, and eventually I became his piano student.

My mother wanted me to have the opportunity to study with different teachers who offered different styles and approaches, and that led her to enroll me at the Beverly Hills Academy of Music. I was nervous at first, because of the very polished wood floors,

sparkling mirrors, professional environment, the seriousness of the teachers, and the competiveness of the other students.

I had lessons every day after school, sometimes into the early evening, and all day Saturday. I moved from ballet to tap, jazz, and interpretive dance. Over time, voice and acting lessons were added. The regimen kept my mind sharp and my growing body strong.

Nothing but dancing mattered in my life. Since I had always been painfully shy, and had a fear of speaking

Modern Dance- age 13;
Weight: 78 lbs. Height
58 inches; Blue-green
eyes: Long brown hair.

Age 11. Doreen Tracey, left, was a fellow Mouseketeer in 1956.

up, dance was a wonderful way for me to express myself without ever having to utter a word.

There aren't enough superlatives to fully describe my dance training. I had the best teachers, and boy, they were strict. They were really Old World in their attitude. Definitely European and definitely from another era! It was clear, even to the youngest students that our teachers knew what they were talking about. And in turn, we gave them our best, exceeding even our own sense of limitations. And it all started with the simplest idea of all: breathing! Imagine that being something you had to learn. And yet, the dancer must be aware of everything!

We were never pampered. Never once did a teacher say to me, "Don't worry. You'll get it next time." Their method was "Now! Do it again. Right now! Don't wait until next time. Maybe there won't be a next time!" They stressed discipline above all else.

How would I describe discipline? My teachers insisted, "Turn your leg. Do it until you get it right.

Look beautiful and very important... REMEMBER TO BREATHE." I became a very good dancer with tremendous leaps and jumps.

My career was made possible, in part, thanks to my wonderful teachers over the years: Michael Panaieff, Val Frohman, Robert Rossellot, Irina Kasmovska, and George Balanchine, creator of the incomparable New York City Ballet. Dancing for him in *The Nutcracker* is something I could have never anticipated...a dream come true.

When I was 14, my mother and I traveled to New York City to see the original cast of *West Side Story* on Broadway. I was thrilled, captivated, inspired, and overcome with emotion. I could see nothing else but dancing and performance in my future. I've never looked back.

Age 15. My father took this photo in front of our Hollywood home.

CHAPTER THREE

Mr. B and Peter and Me in *The Nutcracker Suite*

Recognized as the father of American ballet, George Balanchine was one of the 20th century's most prominent choreographers. He was a choreographer known for his musicality. Balanchine took the standards and technique from his time at the Imperial Ballet School in Russia. He fused them with other schools of movement that he had adopted during his tenure on Broadway and in Hollywood, creating his signature "neoclassical style,"

Arts patron Lincoln Kirstein invited Balanchine to America in 1933, and together they founded The School of American Ballet. Along with Kirstein, Balanchine co-founded the New York City Ballet.

With his School of American Ballet, New York City Ballet, and 400 choreographed works, Balanchine transformed American dance and created modern ballet, developing a unique style with his dancers, highlighted by brilliant speed and attack.

At age 11, my dancing school invited me to audition for George Balanchine and the New York City Ballet.

In New York in 1954, Balanchine premiered *The Nutcracker* by Peter Ilyich Tchaikovsky. An overwhelming success, the ballet still plays there every year.

During that first historic run, Balanchine accepted an invitation to perform his masterpiece at the Greek Theater in Hollywood in the summer months.

Autographed photo of
Balanchine from the 1954 New
York City Ballet program.

The adult dance company, assistant choreographers and all costumes, including the children's costumes, traveled to Hollywood.

Several hundred kids showed up for the auditions. I got to dance personally for Balanchine and he chose me on the spot! There were thirty kids in the company. During the auditions, Balanchine showed us what he wanted. Along with his assistant, Vida Brown, we were taught the routines. We were given 16 to 32 bars of dance. I still remember the steps after all this time. We stood and watched, and then practiced what we had just seen. We practiced and danced, practiced and danced.

I actually felt that it was just me, Mr. B and Peter Ilych dancing together for the entire world to see. What a trio we made!

That first year during the Hollywood run, I danced with the soldiers in their balletic fight with the mice.

The company was huge. Ninety dancers in all with a fifty-piece symphony orchestra performing Tchaikovsky's *Nutcracker Suite*.

At the time of my first audition, I didn't know anything about the *Nutcracker Suite*. All I remember was that I couldn't get the music out of my head. Those gorgeous melodies. To me, music made the dance. It was so complete. Just watching the company during rehearsals, I could hear it and feel it, even the rests and turns. They coursed through me, dancing in time with my heartbeat.

Since the children's costumes were already made, a vital requirement was that we had to fit into the costumes from the New York City production.

The adult company had already performed in New York. But the kid's cast in Hollywood didn't know a thing when we started.

I danced on stage twice during the performance. In addition, I sang with a special group of kids during the "Dance of the Snowflakes." We stood backstage, gathered around a microphone, accompanied on a grand piano. I heard myself singing out loud, full voice, realizing for the first time, that I really didn't have to be as quiet as a church mouse at all. In fact, I could roar!

Dancing celebrities Maria Tallchief, Patricia McBride, Jerome Robbins and Jacques d'Amboise danced in the company. I was dancing with the best dancers in the world! After the performances, I remember running with some of the other young girls to the stars' dressing rooms, asking for toe shoes to keep as souvenirs.

Autographed photo of Jacques d'Amboise from the 1954 New York City Ballet program.

Maria Tallchief: 1954 New York City Ballet Program.

I developed a huge crush on Jacques d'Amboise. Years later, as an adult in Santa Fe, I met him again. He was standing in the lobby of the National Dance Institute, which he had co-founded. I told him about my experience with him at the Greek Theatre and he recalled the Dance Mistress, Vida Brown. I like to think he remembered me, too.

The following summer in 1955, Balanchine invited me to dance with the company during their run of the *Nutcracker* in San Francisco. I danced in the Polichinelles, under the ballerina's huge hoop skirt.

After the *Nutcracker*, my dancing school sent me to another audition, this time for a television show with Eleanor Powell called *Faith of Our Children*. I made the call and the show lasted for nearly a year.

Dancing *Polichinelles* with Elaine Joyce.

CHAPTER FOUR

M-I-C-K-E-Y

WALT DISNEY developed Mickey Mouse in 1928. It was his first highly popular success. He also personally was Mickey's voice until 1947. Originally, Disney named him 'Mortimer' but his wife said that was too pompous and suggested Mickey.

As the studio grew, Walt Disney revolutionized the industry by creating feature-length cartoons in Technicolor. It wasn't until after World War II that Disney introduced live-action films.

In the early 1950's, Disney expanded into the amusement park industry and opened Disneyland. To fund the project, he diversified into television programs: *Walt Disney's Disneyland*, *Davy Crockett*, and of course, *The Mickey Mouse Club*.

Disney chose Bill Walsh to create and develop the show's format. The result was a variety show for children, with such regular features as a newsreel, a cartoon, and a serial, as well as music, talent and comedy features. Mickey Mouse himself appeared in every show. In both the vintage cartoons and in the new animated segments, Mickey was voiced by his creator, Walt Disney.

The Mickey Mouse Club premiered on ABC TV on October 3, 1955.

I was 10 years old when my dad brought home our first TV. He set up the antenna, plugged in the set, turned it on and we were greeted with a scratchy blizzard of gray snow! More fiddling with the set, adjusting the antenna once again, and finally the screen filled with a black and white test pattern- featuring a Native American Indian Chief, in profile.

I was surprised how quickly the industry grew and burgeoned. For me, *The Mickey Mouse Club* was really the beginning of TV.

The year was 1955. Rainbow Studios in Hollywood was the center of my life. All my friends were taking dancing, singing, piano and acting lessons there. Gladys Aherne and her husband managed Rainbow Studios. Syd Tracey taught dance there and I danced with his daughter, Doreen. Like her, I was 12 years old and already a Triple Threat: dancer, singer and pianist.

Disney Studios called and asked the dance studio to send the best dancers to audition for this new show. Doreen and I went and danced together. Doreen made the call and I did not. Of course, I was disappointed,

but took it in my stride... mostly. About ten months later, Mouseketeer auditions were held once again. And once again, a different dance studio sent me to Disney Studios to perform.

A pianist accompanied me and I sang "Over the Rainbow," played the piano and danced. Several of the existing Mouseketeers were on hand for the auditions as well. The choreographer taught us new routines, and evaluated my progress. I was a good dancer and did very well.

When Disney Studios called a few days later with the news of my acceptance, my father insisted, "Go turn on the TV and watch the Mouseketeers." So, I did. I saw the Roll Call and dancing segment and told him, "I can do that!"

My salary was $185.00 per week. An awesome income indeed for a 13-year-old in 1956!

The unsigned contract arrived in the mail. We took the contract into downtown Los Angeles and stood before a Superior Court judge. He reviewed it, and ruled that a certain percentage of my salary was to be deposited by Disney into a special account, and no family member could withdraw that money. That's how things were done with children working in Hollywood at the time. At age 21, I finally collected the money.

The Mickey Mouse Club was filmed at the Disney Studios in Burbank and at Disneyland. I spent a year in that Magic Kingdom. I had no idea how special that year would be.

During the first season and second seasons, the show ran one hour. The show was comprised of individual segments that were put together in the editing room. Each segment ran about four minutes. I spent a lot of time in the sound booth, recording intros for some of the segments.

Talent Round Up Day. I am in the first row between Sharon and Karen.

There was a different theme for each day of the week. Monday was "Fun With Music Day." Tuesday was "Guest Star Day." Wednesday was "Anything Can Happen Day." Thursday was "Circus Day," and Friday was "Talent Round-Up Day."

The show started with Mickey conducting an animated marching band of uniformed mice and Disney characters singing: "Who's the leader of the club that's made for you and me?"

That was followed by a musical introduction and Roll Call by a group of twelve Mouseketeers who introduced themselves by name to the TV audience. Added to the mix were installments of live-action film

serials, cartoons, musical and dance entertainment
and special features.

The whole process was very well managed. The
assistant director handed out individual schedules
every day...starting time and quitting time. A huge
staff of administrators, teachers, social workers,
technicians galore, costumers, makeup artists,
choreographers and cooks were all part of the
Mouseketeam. Our daily assignments were scheduled in many different locations at Disney Studios.
We were all over the place. But the staff kept us orga-
nized and moving. Add to all that three mandatory
hours of schooling each day, sandwiched between
rehearsals and shooting, we had quite an overflowing
schedule. It's a good thing I loved it.

On weekends, Disney TV booked us for special
promotional performances at Disneyland and
other venues like the Hollywood Bowl and the Los
Angeles Coliseum.

The time flew by so fast because we had so much to
do. I don't remember missing a day. It was my job and
I treated it like a job. I was disciplined, as the dancer I
was trained to be.

Disney's version of the 'Little Red Schoolhouse' was where we took classes in red trailers, complete with desks, chairs, blackboards and two teachers. Our group of Mouseketeers ranged in age from 10 to 17.

We studied math, geography and history. That was it! We never left the studio at the end of the day with homework assignments. Instead, we left with scripts. That was our homework. We had to memorize lines, dance steps, and songs.

Our days consisted of three hours of school, one hour for lunch and four hours working on the set. All I wanted to do was to go on stage or do scenes and sing and dance, doing everything I was told to do by the directors, choreographers and stage managers.

After a short time, I became relaxed. Social workers and staff members were there to monitor working, school, and break times. We were escorted to our various assignments on the lot. It was a chopped-up day, but everything somehow ran smoothly.

Every Mouseketeer was required to provide parental guardianship. At the time, my mother was recovering from surgery, so Doreen's mom subbed for her. There were seventeen Mouseketeers and sixteen mothers in our group. Moms were never allowed on the sets or in the classrooms.

There was a movie theater where all the editing was done. Disney provided a small lounge right next to the editing department, which was in the big screen theater. The moms talked and gossiped throughout the day. My mother kept busy with her hands. She sewed little Barbie Doll dresses and outfits. She was quiet and did what she was told by the staff.

In 1956, I was quiet as a mouse: a bit shorter than average, flat as a pancake, with long medium-brown hair.

My first day on the set, the make-up department wound my hair in curlers and gave me a permanent wave, adding curls to the bottom hair only. After the curlers came out, they pulled my hair straight back, revealing my widow's peak, and secured it all with a big barrette. Most of the girls had long hair. Doreen wore two little ponytails. Darlene wore braids. Karen wore Shirley Temple corkscrew curls and Margene had straight long hair, pulled back. We dressed in cotton peddle-pushers, knit short-sleeve turtlenecks and little Mary Jane's with taps, and carried our rehearsal dance shoes with us.

All costumes were made especially for us. The costume department was one of the busiest at the studio. They were always making new costumes. We usually had four or five costume changes per show. All the costumes were relatively simple, but beautifully designed and wonderfully executed.

Throughout the day in different locations, two or three crewmembers each from wardrobe and make-up joined us. They made sure we looked our best and took care of all our individual needs.

The basic Mouseketeer "ears outfit" consisted of a heavy white cotton short-sleeve turtleneck with our name spelled out, each letter individually sewn on. The heavy cotton absorbed sweat during dancing and rehearsals. Blue pleated skirts, blue anklet socks and black tap shoes completed our "uniforms."

We also wore costumes with embroidered aprons, and cowgirl dresses and boots for Talent Roundup Day, as dictated by what the scenes required. I wore Calypso skirts and dresses, evening gowns, bobbysoxer pleated skirts and sweaters.

Originally, Roy Williams, our big grown-up Mouseketeer, who worked as an animator and story man for Disney before the *Mickey Mouse Club*, suggested the cast members wear Mickey and Minnie Mouse Ears. He designed and made the prototypes.

Our Mouseketeer Ears were custom-made. They were lightweight, firmly secured and stayed on through rigorous dance routines and performances. But my ears always seemed crooked. People were always adjusting my ears, but to me they still seemed slightly off center. Maybe it was just my imagination. I guess it fit in with my feelings that I never really did fit in.

Costumes and ears were all property of Disney Studios. We were not allowed to take anything home. And if some part of a costume was lost or damaged, there was a $25.00 replacement fee. I remember Annette lost a set of ears, and yes, she paid the fine. I wish I had the presence of mind to "lose" my ears and pay the fine. I sure would like to have them today.

After the show was over, everything we had remained at Disney, including my ears! As far as I know, they are still there. A few years ago, my girlfriend informed me that my Mouseketeer apron with my name embroidered on front, was auctioned off and sold for $900! I wonder what the iconic ears would bring in at auction?

Walt Disney was on the set for a good part of each day. He was very nice, though a bit reserved. I remember he'd entertain us with card tricks.

I am immediate right – next to Walt Disney!

The directors were adamant that we stay on schedule. We obeyed all rules without question. Every day was different and every day brought new, exciting challenges.

Most of my focus was on the musical segments. The process began in the rehearsal halls...large rooms with mirrored walls and wooden floors. They seemed like big, grown-up versions of the Rainbow Studios and Beverly Hills Academy, where I had started just a few years earlier. We always worked with a pianist and drummer.

Sometimes we received our scripts the night before rehearsal began. Other times we met in the rehearsal halls and started working. We memorized everything by just rehearsing over and over and over.

Most segments consisted of a song and dance number, usually a Judy Garland / Mickey Rooney type.

Tom Mahoney, the choreographer, put together wonderful dance routines for us. We were seventeen dancing Mouseketeers. The choreographer taught us the dance steps, one at a time. It was eight or sixteen bars. Then we would go onto the next sixteen and the next sixteen until the routine was finished. We rehearsed and practiced all day until we mastered it. We'd come back the next day for one more rehearsal. We'd do it once more in costume, then move to the studio and shoot.

As rehearsals continued, I was given more things to do. Sometimes, the kids just jumped into a number and joined the dancing. You jumped in and you either sank or swam. We all swam pretty well. We were talented kids. Sometimes we were asked to sing the music before learning the dance. All songs were performed in the recording studio, for better audio quality. Like dance rehearsals, we sang with a pianist and drummer. The instrumentals were edited in at a different time.

The big challenge was to mime (or lip-sync) the lyrics while we were dancing. The process soon became very natural for me. We were all right on.

CHAPTER FIVE

Hey, I'm a Mouseketeer!

So, what was life like as a Mouseketeer? My first few days in the studio were terrifying. I had never been on a sound stage before. Bells were ringing. And some guy was always yelling "QUIET" at the top of his lungs.

My first day of shooting with the Mouseketeers, I was thrown into a costume and placed on the set. I had no idea what was going on. I was not in the main part of the number. Just in the background. I found it all fascinating. The bells started ringing and it was time to film.

Every minute of the day was filled up. We marched into one studio or another. Nothing seemed out of the ordinary to me because I did it every day. I was doing what I loved to do.

Jimmie Dodd was truly our 'leader of the club!' His formal title was "Official Mouseketeer." Jimmie wrote most of the songs on the show. His tunes contained positive messages for kids. He often provided short segments encouraging young viewers to make the right moral choices. These little homilies became known as "Doddisms." In addition to his other musical contributions, is a song that a generation of kids used for nearly half a century to spell E-N-C-Y-C-L-O-P-E-D-I-A!

Jimmie knew I played piano and especially welcomed me to the Mouseketeers. I think he was one of the reasons I got into the group.

Each show contained a specially choreographed dance number with special costumes and music.

Cubby, Jimmie
Dodd and
Karen. I am
playing piano.

I am far right
with Cheryl
and Lonnie.
Jimmie is
accompanying
us on his
Mouseguitar.

Guest Star Day

On Guest Star Day, I worked with great entertainers of the day, like Leo Carrillo and Judy Canova.

Jerry Lewis and his sons visited the set one day and invited all the Mouseketeers to his house for a birthday party. My sister Harriet drove to his house in Pacific Palisades. We knocked on the door and Jerry answered, and personally escorted us to the swimming pool. We jumped in the pool and had a grand old time.

Almost all the stars we worked with were very giving of themselves. The directors...not so much!

The Talent Roundup

Talent Roundup Day was usually reserved for kids with special talent, but in my season, two of our guests were Fess Parker and Buddy Ebsen, also known as Davy Crockett and George Russell.

I remember doing a scene with Fess Parker. He was dressed in his official Davy Crockett costume, and

With the great Leo Carrillo. I am seated on the bench beside Leo.

we were in our cowboy and cowgirl outfits. Before
the director yelled "QUIET," Fess Parker gathered the
Mouseketeers and told us, "Don't be afraid! You don't
have to worry about anything. If we don't get it in one
take, we'll get it in another." We were all so relaxed
and did the scene in just a few takes. My God, he *was*
Davy Crockett!

Also, on Talent Roundup Day, I got to play host to
Ron Steiner, a Mouseketeer in the first season, who
left the show to return to rejoin his siblings in a dance
act called the Steiner Brothers. They later danced on
the *Ed Sullivan Show*.

Circus Day

On Circus Day, the Mouseketeers hosted a number
of circus acts such as clowns, jugglers and acrobats.
Now, sixty years later, some of my best-remembered
rehearsals involved animals. We were rehearsing a
number for Circus Day featuring the Mouseketeers
and a whole bunch of chimpanzees.

I was standing off to the side watching the
rehearsal and one of the chimps broke loose from
the trainer and ran directly to me. He grabbed my
leg and started sucking on my knee. He didn't hurt
me, but sure scared the hell out of me. The rehearsal
abruptly stopped and several people ran over and
pulled the chimp off my knee. I was left with a huge
blood blister.

Rehearsal resumed and the chimp ran right back to
me and started sucking on my knee again. And again!
Chimpanzee karma, I guess. One of the makeup ladies
rushed to my side and whispered in my ear, "Be brave
and don't be afraid of the chimp or they might cut you
out of the scene. Sit there and take it!"

A few weeks later, we worked on a segment with
a live piglet. Remembering the chimp incident, the

director yelled to me, "You're not going to be scared of a pig, are you?" He was really nasty. And I was really embarrassed.

Fun with Music Day

This was the Mouseketeers' favorite day because we got to sing and dance as a team, and I danced in a lot of "Fun with Music Day" segments. I danced the "Sweet Shoppe Rock," a Calypso Rock. I sang "I'm Biding My Time" with a group of hoboes in "The Tramps." I even danced around a horse and buggy in "Horseless Carriage."

The "Sweet Shops" were interesting. Titled "1925 Sweet Shop," these were a whole series of dances from different eras.

My Turn on Fun with Music Day

My starring role and favorite performance piece was in a "Fun with Music Day" segment titled "The Basketball Ballet." Although a lot of the Mouseketeers played

Late 1800s: Dancing with Lonnie Burr - right.

Still dancing with Lonnie Burr - right.

musical instru-
ments, I was one
of the few who
got an opportu-
nity to solo on
the show.

I was invited
up to the stu-
dio's "Executive
Towers" for a
story confer-
ence with the
director and
choreographer.
The choreog-
rapher wanted
to feature my

Sweet Shoppe close-up.

talent on the piano. It was the first and last time I was
ever asked to visit those hallowed offices. My body was

The Tramps- I sang "Bidin' My Time!" - I am left front.

shaking while I travelled the halls. But I was determined to carry off the role of a professional. I stood
in front of the director's office door, and took a deep
breath before entering. The director was lying on a
lounge and the choreographer was sitting on the desk
facing the piano that was in the room.

The whole show would be based on my idea of being
in a dream-sequence, seated at a majestic grand piano,
dressed in a formal gown.

I was asked to sit down at the piano and play some
jazz...if I could. I replied that all I knew was a little bit
of boogie-woogie. I started to play it and then stopped
in the middle and told them I would rather play something classical, like Beethoven.

All the while I was discussing the story conference
and playing the piano, the director was playing with
himself. I tried to ignore this as best I could. "Maybe
it's a long scratch?" I thought to myself. Anyway, it was
there, right in front of me. Nothing was ever said then,
or remembered. That was my "Me Too!" moment.

In any event, I played the entire piece in one take. The segment was to run eight minutes. It began with the girls practicing ballet in a studio. I was the rehearsal pianist. Enter boy Mouseketeers clad in basketball shorts and

Holiday in Hawaii- I am upper left corner. Cheryl Holdridge is in the foreground.

shirts, dribbling and dancing with the ball. It was a three-minute dance segment with boys and girls challenging each other for floor space.

At the end, there was talk about a big show on Friday night. Everyone was invited but Cubby and me. Cubby was too short for the team. He was wearing a "Mascot" sweatshirt. I wasn't invited because everyone wanted to hear boogie-woogie and I only played the classics! I played a few bars, sighed in dismay, and started playing Beethoven's Für Elise.

While talking to Cubby, I wore a dark jumper and white blouse. There was a close-up of my hands on the keyboard. Fade out. Fade in and my dream began: I was dressed in a beautiful pink frilly evening gown, my hair done up in curls, wearing a gorgeous strand of pearls and high heels. Another close-up shot of my hands! Fade out at the end and I'm back in my jumper and white blouse.

The Land of Me-Oh-My! I am far left.

Für Elise.

All the Mouseketeers were standing around, enraptured by *Für Elise*. I played the final notes to enthusiastic applause. Cubby and I high-fived each other, winked and we all walked off stage. It was my own show!

"Basketball Ballet" aired December 31, 1956, filmed in low-definition, glorious black-and-white.

Anything Can Happen Day (Newsreels)

Truthfully, Anything Can Happen Day was a convenient place to put anything that didn't fit with the themes of the other days. A lot of it was promos. A lot of it was informative or even educational. This was in the days before Sesame Street.

'Newsreels' were 5-minute segments of noteworthy and newsworthy subjects shot on location. Four Mouseketeers interacted with the guest star or educator. In addition to performing, I landed the job of doing all the voice-overs in the recording studios back at Disney Studios.

Voice-overs consisted of an unseen voice narrating the scene. The director wanted a female narrator, and it seems the other Mouseketeer-femme had a lisp.

I worked on two Disneyland newsreels. The first, "Fun with a Camera" was shot at the San Diego Zoo. Our entourage consisted of four Mouseketeers and their mothers, the director, assistant director, makeup and costuming crew, a slew of technicians with cameras. We stayed at the San Diego Traveler's Inn. I thought it was the Taj Mahal.

Earl Tyson was the chief photographer for *Look* magazine. His amazing and insightful photos earned him many awards. He put cameras in our hands and we strolled through the San Diego Zoo taking photographs. It truly was exciting! Most of the segment was shot without sound. I did all of that in the recording studio after the location shoots were done.

The assistant director who came with us accidentally grabbed the wrong dress from the costume department. He took Sharon's dress and she was smaller. My mother came to the rescue and let out

Disneyland series. I am far left. Kevin
Corcoran aka "Moochie" is far right.

With Earl Tyson at the San Diego Zoo.

seams and re-hemmed the dress. All by hand. And in two seconds flat!

The second newsreel, "Rookie Fireman" was filmed at the central fire station in downtown Los Angeles. We were there for a week. We learned the arduous training that firemen have to undergo to prepare for their work.

The grand finale featured me being rescued from a burning house by a fireman on a ladder, and carried down. This was all done on a set. The house set afire was a real concrete building. The façade was lined with asbestos and then really and truly set on fire! The fireman, dressed in his full emergency outfit, rushed onto the set carrying his ladder. After positioning it, he climbed up about 10 rungs, pulled me through the window, and carried me down. What I remember most was not being scared. I was just doing what I was told. And I knew the fire wasn't really out of control.

Left to Right: Charley Laney, Los Angeles County Fire Chief, Keith E. Klinger, Eileen Diamond, Sherry Allen, Walt Disney, Jack Jackman.

Weighing 78 pounds, I was a natural for this role. Filmed at Los Angeles Fire Station Training Ground.

Rookie Fireman. I am in the center between two firemen.

Getting to Know the Mouseketeers

I was hired for the second season. The choreographer wanted more dancing and hired four dancers. I could also sing really well and was unafraid to sing, unlike so many other dancers. Since I was an experienced dancer, I was cast in lots of episodes of the show.

It's incredible that the show has been so vividly remembered by so many generations of families over the years. Like everything, there were the insiders and the outsiders. During my tenure, Annette, Karen and Cubby were the favorites.

We were not at all judgmental of each other. We were too focused on getting it right and standing out for our talent, not for backbiting and jealousies. Most of us were multitalented. Bobby Burgess could do anything. He was an extraordinary dancer, and an incredible cyclist! He honed those skills at the Disney Studios.

My friendship with Doreen Tracey went way, way back to Rainbow Studios. We were great friends at the Disney Studios. Doreen could sing, dance and do comedy, but if I could describe her personality in one word, it would be *impulsive*.

One day she walked over to me during a rehearsal break and said, "I can't be friends with you anymore!"

"Why?" I asked.

"Because you're Jewish and the Jews killed Jesus Christ!"

I was so naïve and stupid. I replied, "Who's Jesus Christ?"

What struck me as funny was that Doreen was half-Jewish on her father's side. Looking back, I knew all the music, lyrics and dance, but I didn't know Jesus Christ. I was truly the naïve Mouseketeer.

When a producer or director crossed paths with us, some of the kids would instantly perk-up and say, "Hello!" The pretty blonde Cheryl Holdridge would get right in their faces.

I never liked competition and shied away from selling myself. Later, I realized that Cheryl was right-on. I should have gone out of my way to say hello to everybody. But that's just not who I was, then or now.

Of course, Annette was definitely the most popular. She starred in a beach blanket series of movies as well as TV and serious dance movies. In the early 1960's I danced with Annette in Disney's "Babes in Toyland."

Annette was the sweetest person I have ever met. She truly loved everybody and I loved her.

Annette "developed" first. Some little bulges were noticeable in her sweater when she was dancing. The wardrobe department strapped her in with Ace Bandages, which I thought was cruel, especially since I didn't have a similar problem. But, for most of us more "typical" girls, developing was not a problem. We were flat-chested but sang and danced like big-busted professionals.

With the exception of Annette, I never worked with any of the old Mouseketeers after the show was over. None of them went on dance calls, which were part of my daily life.

I did run into Bobby Burgess in the late 1960s. My husband Roy and I were vacationing at Crater Lake National Park in Oregon. We said a quick "hello!" He told me that he was losing his dancing partner on *The Lawrence Welk Show* and asked if I was interested! I said, "No thanks." At that time, being married seemed more important to me than being a dancer on a TV show.

On some weekends, the Mouseketeers were sent out to work special appearances.

Most vividly, I remember our show for The Boy Scouts of America. The Los Angeles Coliseum was

Back stage at the Hollywood Bowl (Eileen in third row on right).

packed with more than 80,000 scouts and parents. I had never seen so many kids before. They were all screaming and hollering for our autographs. I couldn't believe that an audience that size could get so worked up.

I had no concept of "celebrity" and didn't feel like a "star." Everybody was screaming and idolizing us. Maybe we *were* famous!

There were lots of changes going on around us during the second full year of the *Mickey Mouse Club*. There would be a third season shrunk down to thirty minutes, and the show's fourth year consisted of re-mixes from the first two years. That means they took film sections from popular shows and edited them into new shows. Years later, there was a lawsuit about their doing that. But Disney and his lawyers won. No more royalties for us. Some of us were asked back to do some voice-overs in the sound studio, but I was not.

My contract expired at the end of the second season and I wasn't asked back for the third. I was shocked and disappointed. I called Doreen Tracey with the news.

"That's show business." she replied.

Ouch!

About 10 years after the show ended, Roy Williams, the biggest Mouseketeer, hosted a reunion at his home in the Valley. That's where I rekindled my friendship with Mouseketeer Judy Harriet. She left at the end of the first season as I was coming in.

There were several informal Mouseketeer reunions over the years. Some were held at Disneyland and others at private homes. However, in 1980, an all-out, grand TV reunion was planned to celebrate and commemorate 25 years since the *Mickey Mouse Club* debuted.

I was living in Palm Springs at the time, married with two kids, and carrying about 10 extra pounds.

But I managed to shed the pounds before driving into Los Angeles for the reunion. I didn't want to be the only Mooseketeer!

Twenty of the thirty-nine original Mouseketeers showed up! My initial reaction was positive. I definitely wanted to dance and don my "Ears" just one more time.

It was a little unsettling to see the Mouseketeers were all grown up. In my mind's eye, we were still teenagers singing and dancing for the cameras. But here we were, adults, working with new directors and choreographers, learning brand new dance routines, just like the old days.

In the late '70s, most of the Mouseketeers were still living and working in Hollywood, while I had been living in Paris with my family.

We had moved there when my husband, Roy became partners with the Academy Award-winning composer, Michel Legrand and we moved to Europe so he could

My son, Joshua, is sitting on the trunk in the CAMP tee shirt. Daughter Shahna with the long braid is standing and I am the beaming Mommy Mouseketeer far right. Annette is second left, Judy Harriet is between us with her daughter, Lisa. Bonni Kern is at the left with her daughter, Kim.

head up their international production company. I realized how my life was different from the others.

The Mickey Mouse Club 1980 Reunion was truly the first time I realized that I was no longer a child TV personality. I had finally grown-up to become a wife and mother, and I loved it. I was able to look back on my Mouseketeer years with fondness- and perspective.

Thoughts Along the Way
A Reflection on
Performance and Fear of Failing
written in the early 1970s

I've always been a loner and an introvert. I was never an outspoken person. Even the publicity note next to my name, Eileen Diamond, on the old Mouseketeer roster says, "She is a quiet girl." I was afraid to say a word for fear it might be held against me.

Why do I have to prove myself to others, when inside I know it's all there? Wait a minute, maybe if I was really self-confident and had it all together, I wouldn't have to try and make myself known or prove myself. Obviously, my shrink, or any doctor, hears this all the time. If people applaud you then you can accept yourself. If other people say you are good, then you must be. It is the written or spoken word, like actors living for their reviews, yearning to be liked.

It all ties in doesn't it? I call this "munum theory." It's almost as clear as a reward system for a Pavlovian dog theory. One likes a pat on the head and you say "munum munum" like petting a dog. In other words, we all need feedback. But in order to get feedback, one must do something in the first place

One sign of a good director is to give encouragement where it is needed. There was so much competition going on between all the kids and so much trying to please the director and producers. In retrospect there was constant pushing and upstaging wherever possible. It made me ill.

Quiet outside, but roaring inside! That's it! The Mouseketeer that Roared. Finding my voice for all to hear. At last! It was a long way from sitting with my two-year old daughter, Shahna, innocently watching the opening episode of *The Mickey Mouse Club*. Memories swelled up into my eyes. Her question was "Where are you Mommy?"

There I was as big as life telling my daughter "That's me when I was a little girl." Some little! I was thirteen.

Walking into Disney Studios was like a fairy tale for me. Perhaps I *was* living out a fantasy. I sang my rear end off, danced my heart out and even played the piano. They loved it.

And now it's just me and this page you are reading.

All of a sudden, I'm intimidated. There's a blank piece of paper staring at me, with my notes at my side... pictures of my young life...episodes of all that I had been and had become.

So, what is the secret of happiness? Of course there is no answer. I would be naive to try and put it down on paper. No answer exists. It's just what you yourself bring to your own life, how you write your own history, once you get through all the bad habits and obstacles you build for yourself.

I began to understand that the auditions I made or didn't make, did not define who I was. Too often, they were about appearance...not who I was, but how I looked.

Disney did not pick up my contract. Try to explain that to a thirteen-year-old. Not having my contract renewed is a euphemism for being rejected or fired in our business.

As I'm sitting here writing, I'm thinking of the encouragement I get from my husband. I really don't ask for it, but I sort of want him to know I did it on my own.

My mother devoted her life to my life of performance. Even in later years she managed to fly from one place to another to see me perform. We loved each other dearly. She lived her whole life for me, nothing for herself. After I was married, and then years later after I had my first child, there was more and more of a separation between us.

I was going over some old documents, contracts and newspaper clippings, and came across a 1956 *TV Guide*. There was an article in it where one of the directors of the Mouseketeers show said that all of us were chosen for our personalities and talents, and had no ambitions to go further with our careers. Funny, he was so close, but couldn't see the forest for the trees, or the individuals in the chorus.

No, we were not judgmental of each other and tried to do our best, but still the competition ran high. One girl went around yodeling all day, long hoping she would get a solo spot in one of the many songs we sang in the show. Another girl made sure she said a bubbly "Hello!" complete with fluttering eyelashes, to anyone who seemed they might be able to put her in the front row.

When we did group scenes, the pushing to be out front was debilitating. There was even a time when we were told to choose our partners and I ran to Bobby, one of the best male dancers, to be my partner, and was told by one of the other girls that he belonged to her exclusively! I didn't give up though. That was one of the first times I ever stood my ground. Too bad I didn't learn from that experience to always stand up for myself. That took decades.

These stories all seem so petty now. They were important to me at the time, though. I did have one person in my corner all the time. He was our choreographer, a good person and very talented man, Tom Mahoney. I will never forget the trust and confidence he had in me.

Sometimes your head gets in the way of your feet. Insecurity is the enemy of talent. And talent, by itself, isn't enough. Encouragement is always the motivator, but sometimes with a catch. If I had one choreographer rooting for me I had one director thinking I was a pain in the ass.

Words and Music
written in 1978

Dear Book,

So, what do I do now? I have to make you bigger and longer and better, and who knows what else to make sure my voice speaks from every page.

Walt Disney was an amazing man. We saw glimpses of him when he was working on another set introducing his new "Disneyland" series. He wanted to be known to the public. He furthered the Disney image with everything he touched. The movie classics he made go on and on. They are timeless. And so is he.

In the mid 1950's there was a large void in children's television programming. In fact, there was precious little programming for children at all. We were long before the days of *Mr. Roger's Neighborhood* and *Sesame Street*, to say nothing of *Nickelodeon*. Disney paved the way for television entertainment created especially for children.

The hard work that was expected of us didn't bother us. We all loved it. It certainly wasn't a "normal" childhood. I don't even remember being young. We lived in a world of television cameras, directors and choreographers, and the imaginary world that Disney had created.

It was as if time had stopped, and those years became frozen in the minds of generations to come. Maybe this is why I had so much trouble breaking out of my shell in later years. I was paid to be defined by my dancing and singing. We weren't in school, interacting with other students, learning from them and experiencing all the things that are part of growing up. Those opportunities came later. The Mouseketeers and I had a lot of catching up to do.

There were secret lunches some of the kids were invited to behind the commissary's closed doors. I never knew if Disney was there or just some producers showing off their little creations up close and personal to the sponsors they were trying to woo.

It was an eerie feeling walking onto the set where I had worked perhaps twenty years before. Music in the background. Lights and spots and cameras rolling. Assistants and makeup men and hairdressers running around everywhere.

Choreographers screaming and directors saying "Do it again. Watch your blocking. You're in the wrong place. Move to the left a little. No, too far. Back one step!" Just like the old days

For what and for whom? Then I came back to reality. It wasn't me out there. I was twenty years older now, watching a new generation of Mouseketeers. I was one of the originals. And I had been one of them. That little thirteen-year-old ball of energy and talent, singing, dancing and smiling her way into the hearts of countless kids all over the country watching her on television. We had become friends with thousands of kids who recognized us, welcomed us into their homes.

So much remained the same. The main dancer looked very upset because they made her do it over and over again. How many times can she put on that beautiful smile without looking pained in the face?

"Just one more time" shouts the director. The young girl was about to collapse. Where the hell are the social workers and the teachers to look out for the kids?

I walked around to the back of the set and some mothers pounced on me, discovering that I, too, was once a Mouseketeer. "Do you think they are going to renew the show?" As if I had something to do with that decision. I, who was cut and not renewed so many years earlier! It seemed so ironic. It's as if their child's life were at stake. Did they feel wanted or rejected? Should this have been happening in their lives so soon? Maybe it would prepare them for what's out there later on in life. Oh, I don't know! It still pains me now to see all this responsibility thrust on the young and talented. And nobody really seemed to care for the individuals.

I always felt an obligation to listen and do what I've been told. But, there's more to it than that. You also have to follow your own instincts. No one knows better. When will I learn that? Why am I waiting for everyone else to tell me what I already know? Or should be learning? I always knew how good I was but that wasn't enough. I was always looking for someone else to confirm what I hoped was true. And yet, it was true with or without their approval. I was just never able to trust my own instincts. I, who just wrote that! "You have to follow your own instincts!"

We women are a unique breed. Often, we are stuck in the house with the kids, caring for them, our husbands and our extended families. Little by little, if we are lucky, we peer out from behind the security of our safety net and begin to look at the world outside. We show our faces, little by little. Is anybody there? Does anybody care?

Rests and Remembrances

written in 1980

Where did I leave off? Oh, yes, I'm back from living abroad. Four years living in France was long enough. I did make some wonderful lasting friendships while there. And my mind felt alive and fertile. I created some new writing by myself and with a friend. I was challenged and encouraged as never before.

ON BEING A MOUSEKETEER
I used to think I was just a fly in the ointment, or maybe a mouse with her foot in her mouth. I look at life differently now, with my eyes wide open and my mouth shut.

I was part of an era of television that is long gone. It was a time of awakening for the whole country. A time of losing our idyllic post-war outlook as a nation, and starting to assess what it was going to take to move us forward. Television went from black and white to color. So did our lives.

Before, we didn't have to worry about who shot J.R. It was all we could do to know who Spin and Marty were going to ask to the dance. At the time I was thirteen, very young and impressionable. I thought the whole world was song and dance. It was a beautiful world with the exceptions of learning that some Mouseketeers were created more equal than others and that prejudices did exist.

Just give me a few lines to say, a song and dance routine, and I was on my way, oblivious to it all. A little push and shove here and there, but I made my way and my presence was felt. At least I hoped so.

Where are all the Eleanor Powell's of today? I miss "Singing in the Rain" with Gene Kelly. Are these all times gone by? Is the world getting too complicated to remember the simple things in life? I yearn for the years of black and white.

1980: MOUSEKETEER REUNION THAT ALMOST WASN'T

I received a call from one of the producers of the Mouseketeer 25th Anniversary Reunion show asking if I was still capable of performing. "Of course," I said with great alacrity.

"All right, now I've got to get back into shape! Loose twenty pounds and really dig in at my Dancercise class." I wanted to look beautiful and strut my stuff.

The letters were arriving almost daily from Disney Studios: Be here at such and such a date. Please come with pictures. What size shoes do you wear? Please send resume and recent photo.

I hadn't taken my measurements in years. I used to be a perfect... well, who cares? I'm not anymore!! On the other hand, now I'm just perfect. Wish I could believe that.

All of a sudden, I took it into my head that I should go to see the producers of the show by myself and see if I could be of any help. I write. I produce, and I have so much to give, off stage as well as on.

So off I went with very high expectations to knock them dead with my wit and talent and beauty. (I very seldom say that). Well, I thought I had succeeded. They were impressed and said perhaps I might be one of the lucky nine out of thirty-six who would be the key group around which the whole show would be centered. I went out of there flying high because I thought *finally* after all these years my talents showed through. I wouldn't be pushed in the back and finally make the Roll Call. My dream was shattered when I was finally called back. "We're sorry, but we want to go with the originals... the ones who were on the show for three years."

The big day was approaching. Nine of the other kids had been in rehearsals for two weeks already. I was lucky enough to get two days of work out of it. Judy Harriet was with me. We were known as the "B" group. There were twelve of us, and then there was a "C" group, which consisted of ten more. They only worked for one day.

Judy and I went in a week early to take pictures and see the "A" group rehearsing. They looked like an old chorus line. It was all about Disney, as in hindsight, it should have been. But the lines between Disney and the Mouseketeers blurred, and we thought that it was about us.

What I learned that day was that my whole life was not as a Disney Mouseketeer.

Most of my fears had subsided after my picture call visit the week before. *Time* magazine interviewed us as equals. The reporter talked with me for a longtime. He asked me why we still referred to each other as "kids?" I thought it was a wonderful question.

When the article finally came out there was no mention of me, just the key nine kids with their picture next to an old one that I was in. My name was not in it.

People magazine came out with an article and picture a few weeks later. At least Judy and I made that one. They put the key group in front again. Now, to my surprise, I was the tallest girl.

There was a strike threatened by the Screen Actors Guild. We all knew it, but the producers paid no mind and kept the shooting schedule the same. The SAG strike stepped in and rehearsals stopped. Nothing was filmed and we were all waiting to hear when we could begin again.

We were not allowed to shoot on the Disney lot because of the SAG strike. We were asked to put on our shirts with our names on them. Twenty-five of us showed up.

Off we went on a hot day in a hot bus to a hot photography studio in the middle of a hot summer. Then there was Cubby, who never showed up even though we all waited for him for three sweltering hours. He was stuck somewhere on the road between Las Vegas and LA, where he had just completed playing a show.

The head of publicity for Disney, Arlene Ludwig, said, "OK" for the first shot:

"Let's have all the originals and the key nine kids stand in front."

The photographer arranged all twenty according to importance, with Annette up front and in the middle.

Cheryl got into the first picture even though she wasn't one of the Nine. Sherry got in the picture because she was to be in the key group replacing Doreen. The upper echelon at Disney decided to remove Doreen from the key group because she did a nude layout for a magazine. (That's not very Disney-like). She was awfully sweet when I talked with her. We used to take dancing together in Hollywood at the Rainbow Studios.

Doreen came to the studio with her seventeen-year-old son. The last time I remembered working with her she wasn't even seventeen herself.

Well I finally made it into the picture. The last shot, so to speak, I was way in the back.

We were all part of making television history. Each and every one of us stood out in our own way and with our own particular talents.

Did it teach me a lesson? Many. I wouldn't have changed my experiences for anything, key group or not. The "Nine" were talented yes, but the rest of us were talented, too, if not as popular.

CHAPTER SIX

Israel Tour

Many professional clubs and non-profit organizations in town often called the dance schools and invited their most promising students to perform at their meetings. I performed at a lot of these events, mostly women's clubs, and a lot of Jewish organizations as well. At the time I was studying at the Beverly Hills Academy and shows featuring the young and gifted were considered perfect teatime entertainment.

In 1958 some of the leaders in the Los Angeles Jewish community suggested a visit to the Israeli Consulate. The Nation of Israel was getting ready to celebrate its 10th birthday. Introductions with the Israeli Ambassador were arranged for my parents and me.

We arrived at the Consulate. I came prepared with a show I put together on my own. The theme was American Teenagers, 1958. Mostly I chose jazz dancing and singing, along with some tap. Some of my teachers helped me prepare different routines. I also danced to some Israeli folk music.

The hit of my show was "The Flying Purple People Eater!" Clad all in purple, including purple wig, I tapped and sang the entire song!

Also included in my show were several Israeli folk dances. I choreographed some of my own original steps. I wanted to share my knowledge and appreciation of their culture and music with them, through the eyes of an American teenager.

The Israeli ambassador invited me, accompanied by my parents, of course, to perform my show throughout Israel, as well as several American military bases across Europe.

Our journey began in Paris... and then ended in Paris. It was a thrilling and edifying look at the big world that lay outside the streets and studios of Hollywood.

Both my parents spoke fluent Yiddish and were able to converse easily, especially in Germany where asking for directions was very natural for my dad. Much easier than it was for Mom and me to ask for directions in Paris. We were eager to see the Eiffel Tower and took a cab. We kept repeating "Eiffel Tower!" "Eiffel Tower!" to the cabdriver, who claimed not to understand. Finally, after much pantomime we finally made our point. "Tour D'Eiffel." I think he just wanted us to feel like ugly Americans. Anyway, we finally got there and it was more stunning than we could have ever imagined.

My father purchased a brand new German Borgward automobile before we left the States and we picked it up in Paris, where it became our official transport. I remember my father flying an American flag from the antenna to identify us as Americans and not Germans, in a country, which was still recovering from the War. After the tour was over, the car was shipped back to us in California, where my dad promptly sold it.

We drove across most of the European continent. Driving through Switzerland was my favorite. It absolutely stunned my senses. It was summertime, yet the snow-capped mountains shimmered as they rose from the lush and brilliant green hills. I celebrated my 15th birthday in Venice, about which I only remember the smelly canals and claustrophobic heat. Later on, visiting Venice as an adult, I was able to appreciate the beautiful buildings and art. But the canals were still smelly and the heat oppressive. But this time I was able to get a gondolier to float me down the canals. The serenade I was hoping for never came. Neither did his tip! And the canal still smelled.

We drove through Paris several times. Each time my father tied an American Flag onto the Borgward's antenna! The Cold War was just beginning to thaw-out, but relations between the Germans and French were still tense and my father felt awkward driving a German car.

My father had cousins living in Paris. True to family traditions, his cousin was a tailor. To celebrate the occasion, he made a French suit for me. It was made of brown, heavyweight Berber wool with a short skirt and matching jacket and vest. I was honored and flattered. And hot!

I carried a huge purse throughout the trip, across cities and countries. It was a revelation to find a different country across a border, not just a different state. Each time we dined; I stashed the sugar cubes in my gargantuan purse. As the journey continued, my purse grew heavier. And when we arrived back in Paris for the last time, I gave my French cousin all the sugar cubes, and the bag, too. "How sweet of you," she said, with a knowing smile.

"El-Al" onward and upward! We landed in Tel Aviv just before their tenth anniversary celebrations.

I had learned lots of the history, stories and customs of Jewish life from my Hebrew School education. Imagine, being in the birthplace of my people, a people with a five-thousand-year history. The streets I walked and the sights I saw had been seen by generations and generations that had come before. And, in many cases, nothing had changed.

Our itinerary took us through many kibbutzim: communal farms and industries scattered across the desert terrain. Grandparents, parents and children worked alongside each other, laboring to make their desert land fertile and abundant. I was surprised to see children living in dorms, separately from their parents during the workweek. I watched them plant hundreds of seedlings and I wondered if they might not live to see them grow and flourish. But there was a firm belief that their children would be the beneficiaries of their faith.

I remember standing on the Jordan-Israel border, before the 6-Day War, looking over a fence from the lush green landscape onto the dry and barren Jordanian desert. To this day, Israel is a beacon of agricultural, cooperative living that is a model throughout the world.

The Israelis we met were truly bursting with pride. Kids, just a few years older than I was, were clad in Army gear...boys and girls. Military service was mandatory for both sexes at age eighteen. They were proud and eager to help the country grow and prosper. And that requirement to serve has endured throughout the years.

Everybody in Israel, from farmers to soldiers to kibbutz kids, were picking grapes and grapefruits. Grandparents and parents spoke with pride. "Look at our children," they would say, "They are the future of Israel!"

English was the second language in Israel. It was easy to share stories and exchange ideas. I even started corresponding with a group of boys that continued after I got back to Hollywood.

We stayed beachside in Tel Aviv, right on the Mediterranean shore. The beaches were packed on Saturdays. It was everybody's day off. There were cafes along the beachfront and at night they were bursting with energy... music and dance lighting them up until early the next morning.

1958 aboard the S/S *Liberte*- Returning home after the Israel Tour.

I felt very different when we got back to Hollywood. I saw life in a totally new perspective. Different people, different countries. Threats and pride. A big bold new world.

Shortly after we returned, my aunt Gertrude pinched my cheeks and congratulated me. "You've grown-up so much!" She was kvelling (bursting with pride).

September rolled around and I went back to school at Bancroft Junior High School.

The school administrators thought my greatest potential was in journalism. On the first day of school I asked the journalism teacher to transfer me to the Theater Department. A brilliant move! My acting teacher was the best.

I started my high school years at Hollywood High and transferred mid-way to Fairfax High School. Fairfax had a much better reputation, and I was beginning to think about college.

Even though we were in the heart of Hollywood, I was the only Mouseketeer in any of my public schools.

Nobody had danced, sang, and played piano for millions of kids. Nobody. I was surprised that the kids in my classes weren't even curious about my experiences. My accomplishments abroad didn't impress those Hollywood kids, who were used to living amongst celebrities and movie studios.

I danced in some school productions and choreographed and danced in my own version of George Gershwin's "Rhapsody in Blue" and that led to my being recruited by a girl's club at Fairfax, and I eagerly joined.

I became an official member of the Cubidons. We wore white-buck shoes, which we powdered every evening. White pleated skirts and white blouses. The school did not allow us to wear any make-up, so that was never an issue. We huddled together at school dances and giggled and picked out our own individual Prince Charming. Few, if any, were charming at all. And not a Prince in sight!

CHAPTER SEVEN

Me, Dancing in Pictures

The Mickey Mouse Club enabled me to hone my skills on the small screen. My one-year residence at the Disney Studios was phenomenal. The Israeli and European Tour broadened my world.

During my senior year in high school, I auditioned for Jerome Robbins' film version of "West Side Story." Hundreds of kids showed up. I learned the routines, danced, and got called back for a second interview. I was cut when they learned I was only fifteen. State laws and strict unions demanded the studios hire teachers for all working kids under eighteen. It was cheaper for the studio to hire older kids who didn't need tutors on the set. I would ultimately dance in several films.

My dance background taught me that discipline and responsibility were key components to surviving and flourishing in that very competitive world. So were taking care of your body, keeping up with exercises and dance lessons, and eating and sleeping well. All these were requirements to maintaining a healthy, well-tuned, and flexible body. And it didn't hurt my high kicks or *bat mois* at all. I had to rely on peripheral vision to stay in sync with the other dancers around me. There were no mirrors in the rehearsal rooms.

Having danced on television and on stage, I would learn that dancing in film requires more concentration. The disruption of cutting up the routine into what seems like fifty million shots at different angles, was extremely challenging because there was no sense of continuity. Just another reason why I always preferred live performance to film. Also, I had to face the reality that once this job was over, I had to go out and audition for the next.

There has never been a mandatory retirement age for dancing on the silver screen. Your career was over when you couldn't raise your legs for high kicks!

I was already a Hollywood veteran at sixteen. I knew who rang the bell to "shoot!" and who yelled "QUIET" at the top of his lungs. Working in movie musicals was like the *Mickey Mouse Club* on steroids! Hundreds of people worked behind the scenes. Everyone was friendly and everyone was focused on his or her specific task.

Auditions were quite a different thing from filming. If you've ever seen *A Chorus Line*, then this becomes easy to visualize. Picture eight by ten glossy headshots, representing a real, live, breathing human being yearning to be discovered. A few difficult dance steps being taught in a few intense moments, and then finally it's your turn to shine and make history. Then you hear that terrifying word: "Next!" Not good news. Not good news at all.

We wore leotards and tights, and tried to accessorize and style our hair, make-up, or anything that might draw attention to you—and not someone else. In Hollywood you had to be exactly what they were looking for...not shorter or taller...not blonder or less blond. Just what they wanted, even if they didn't know what that was.

After the director and choreographer typecast you by physical appearance, the next step was to see how you danced.

We were usually called in groups of ten: five in front, five in back. The choreographer's assistant taught us a sequence of steps. First, one step and then another eight bars, and another. We had to learn a whole sequence of dance steps in a very short time. The next group repeated the routine, and so on. It was a process of elimination.

Dancers were not credited in films. Instead we joined a union called the Screen Extras Guild (SEG), which has since merged with the Screen Actors Guild (SAG).

The Screen Extra's Guild notified me for upcoming auditions. I called in each morning to find out what was filming and where.

Other non-credited groups in SEG were "Extras." Literally, they were all the people in each scene without speaking lines and some singers who remained anonymous. On the set, we were known as "Background," or "Atmosphere." I found the terms dehumanizing! It's like playing a tree in your grammar school Christmas show.

If the dance work finished early, I was sometimes called to work as an Extra. I remember working a few dance steps on a film with Ann Margaret. I don't remember the name of the film or my role name. Just "Atmosphere."

A movie job could last two weeks or a month. Obviously, the longer the better. We mastered the dance numbers from beginning to end. Some film crews shot the full number as a reference for the editor, who would then review it to make choices and corrections as needed.

Then the editor, director, and choreographer watched the dancers rehearse the number live. They'd break it apart and put it back together again: several times, if necessary. Time to move from the rehearsal halls to the studio to shoot!

Shooting took another week or two. We just worked on individual segments with no rhyme or reason, not necessarily in running order. It all seemed very random. I'm sure it had to do with location, scenery, costumes, story, cast and lots of other important elements. But I just found the process time-consuming and boring. If we weren't in a specific segment, we had to just sit around and wait. Be there. Be ready. Be prepared... and wait. The cameras and tech crew were between us and the dance being filmed, and completely blocked the real action. It was hard to see anything. And we had to be very quiet. Doesn't sound glamorous, does it? Well, it wasn't, but it required a high degree of professionalism.

All the magic took place in the editing room. Somehow, the editors created the flow of the first run-through, but with close-ups, costume changes and overhead shots. The only glimpse of the movie I got was with my dancing group in the studio. I had no idea what was going on with anything except what we were rehearsed to do. The storyline, shooting schedule, design and overview were completely alien to us. We simply weren't part of all that.

Atmosphere. That's what we were. Sometimes dancing or singing atmosphere, but atmosphere, nonetheless. And we were lucky to be involved. There were always plenty of aspiring young performers waiting in line to replace us if we faltered.

Everyone was busy doing their work in their particular area. The dancers were off practicing their steps. The singers were learning their music, and the actors were off somewhere else, memorizing lines and blocking (positioning).

My focus was always on preparation and performance. There wasn't much time for recreation. I was always dead tired when I got home at night.

We were out of there as soon as our dance was done filming. No fanfare, just back to lining up dance calls for future auditions.

We were paid for rehearsal times and shooting. We were also paid for wardrobe calls. We had to report to the wardrobe department for individual fittings. The process usually took a few hours. The patterns were pinned on us, measurements taken, notations made, and costumes sewn.

Make-up and hair styling were the first steps in the process, followed by dressers from the wardrobe department who carefully dressed each one of us individually.

The costumes were magnificent... a far cry from the plain, white knit Mouseketeer turtlenecks and pleated skirts.

A bright side was that I got to meet and work and dance with some incredible choreographers like Bob Fosse and Jerome Robbins from the Broadway stage. I also worked with cinema choreographer legends Hal Belfer, Onna White, Dee Dee Woods and her partner Tom Panko. And of course, Tom Mahoney, with whom I worked on the Mickey Mouse Club.

I still remember the thrill of auditioning for Gene Kelly at MGM when I was just six years old! I worked at all the major film studios during my career. Each studio had its own mark and take on things.

The streets of the Disney Studio were named after cartoon characters. For example, there was the corner of Mickey Mouse Boulevard and Donald Duck Avenue. It was hard not to feel like a family pet or zoo creature. Twentieth Century Fox was the opposite. It was beyond huge and totally impersonal. It just kept rolling on for miles through West Los Angeles.

In addition to the movies, I worked on a few episodes of the TV show, *Route 66*. I was a professional extra on some episodes filmed at the beach. I got the job because I looked good in a bikini, flat-chested though I was. I danced, bikini-clad, with a group of hippies and beach bums.

I also picked up a few random jobs with local Hollywood companies that were not part of the studios.

CAM Records (Choreography and Music) recorded musical soundtracks and attached photos of dancers highlighting individual dance positions. These packages were intended for dancers to hear the musical cues and learn the sequences and steps. I worked on several of these albums.

Scopitone was another dancing venture for me. A Scopitone was a type of jukebox that featured a 16 mm film component with a video screen mounted on top. Color filmstrips with magnetic soundtracks were viewed and heard. In a sense, this was a precursor to music videos and MTV.

Presents . . .

MISS EILEEN DIAMOND

Eileen began dancing at the age of 5 and has been, ever since a 'trouper' in the truest sense of the word. While dancing is her first love, this multi-talented teenager has proven her versatility by carrying off a number of varied assignments as a dancer, singer, actress, pianist, and model with all the poise and consummate skill of the true professional.

As the protegé of Bobby Davis, top choreographer for C.A.M. Records, Eileen has most recently made several appearances with Mr. Davis as his assistant, demonstrating his routines. Her past credits include a highly successful year as a member of the famed Walt Disney's Mouseketeers; 2 seasons (summers of '54 & '55) with the New York City Ballet, at the Greek Theatre in Los Angeles Griffith Park, and the San Francisco Opera House, receiving special praise for her dancing in the 'Nutcracker Suite' with that company; plus several fine parts in stage. Radio & T.V. plays. She is leaving soon, with her parents for a tour thru Europe to Israel, and is slated for several personal appearances on this trip.

Eileen, thru all this, has maintained her sweet and completely natural personality and is today an unassuming and studious young lady. We at C.A.M. Records are proud of her association with us, and we are sure, once you have seen her, you will believe as we do; that Eileen Diamond is destined to be one of the brightest stars of the entertainment world.

Debbie Reynolds was one of the first investors to bring Scopitone to the U.S. By 1966, nearly a thousand Scopitones were installed in bars and restaurants across the country.

The biggest musical stars of the 1960s never performed on Scopitone. However, several well-known acts were featured. I was in a number called "If I Never Get to Heaven," with Della Reese and another with Bobby Vee (again in a bikini) singing "Baby Face."

Filmwork

I'm proud to have been part of these films, not to mention having my teen years preserved for posterity!

The Music Man

The Music Man was based on the 1957 Broadway smash hit. It was filmed at the Warner Brothers Studio in 1961 and released in 1962. The film was nominated for six Oscars and won "Best Musical Score" for Ray Heindorf. Morton DaCosta, who directed the show onstage in New York. He not only directed the film, but produced it as well, ensuring the film was faithful to the show.

Robert Preston scored a great success as Harold Hill on Broadway. Jack L. Warner, who was notorious for wanting to film stage musicals with stars other than the ones who played the roles onstage, wanted Frank Sinatra for the lead role, but composer Meredith Wilson, insisted on Preston. Warner also "begged" Cary Grant to play Hill, but Grant declined saying, "nobody could do the role as well as Bob Preston."

The film made Robert Preston an "A" list star in motion pictures, after appearing in supporting roles most of his career. In 2005, *The Music Man* was selected for preservation in the United States National Film Registry by the Library of Congress as being "culturally, historically, or aesthetically significant."

The first dance calls went out in early 1961. I was still in high school, but getting ready to graduate. After a few months into the process, several dancers had to be replaced due to injuries. A second dance call was announced about six months later, and I was hired. I was sixteen and a high school grad.

I worked on the set for about three weeks, dancing first in the bleachers of the high school gym, and then marching outside behind Robert Preston, who was dancing and playing an imaginary trombone. Warner Brothers brought in local school bands for the scene and it was one of the most memorable images in any film.

I was also cast as an "extra" for a classroom scene. I had no lines to speak, but hung around the classroom until the doors flew open and then I ran into the gym and started dancing on the bleachers, and singing "76 Trombones" at the top of my lungs. We had much more fun than the kids who spoke a few lines but weren't cast in that legendary number. Those who spoke lines were from different unions with different protocols to follow.

Onna White was the choreographer. The kids in our number worked with her assistants, Dee Dee Woods and Tommy Panko. No scripts were issued to us because we were dancers and didn't have any lines. We were assigned rehearsal times and learned the routines. The dance steps we did mimicked the imaginary instruments we were playing. We rehearsed in a practice studio and after we learned all the pieces, we spent another two- or three-weeks filming.

There were a lot of segments to learn because we moved from inside the gym onto the streets, and danced our way across most of the Warner Brothers Studio lot. And we danced the last few minutes in formal band uniforms! There was no live band to accompany us, so we danced to recorded music. We didn't have to sing, but everybody was dancing.

There were some other musical dance numbers with kids, but they were cast before I made became available for the second dance call.

All told, our group numbered close to a hundred. Dancers, choreographers, techs, costumers, make-up men and women, directors, stagehands... the list went on and on. Food trucks followed us from location to location, feeding us coffee, lunch and snacks. It was one of the few times in Warner history that we were allowed to eat in our costumes, which was usually forbidden.

I don't recall too much direct contact with the film's stars, but their presence and personalities were infectious, lifting us to great heights as young performers.

Shirley Jones had just won the Oscar for Best Actress in *Elmer Gantry*. I remember she brought the esteemed statue to the set, and we all got an up-close and personal exchange with Oscar himself.

Robert Preston was truly a bigger-than-life leading man because he "owned" the role of the Music Man, and Meredith Wilson, its creator, would not hear of anyone else doing it.

Buddy Hackett was the opposite of Robert Preston's charm and congeniality. He was a foul-mouthed human being, who relished groping and poking. He groped and poked as many chorines as possible.

I worked with a very young Ronny Howard during the filming. We played card games together. Ronny was seven years old. He played Marion's baby brother, Winthrop Paroo and sang two big songs from the show, "Gary Indiana" with Robert Preston, and "The Wells Fargo Wagon." All with a believable lisp! And from that young star came "Happy Days" and ultimately, one of the most prolific and successful directors in Hollywood.

Babes in Toyland

Babes in Toyland was a 1961 Walt Disney musical set for Christmas release. It starred Ray Bolger as the villain Barnaby, Annette Funicello as Mary Contrary, Tommy Sands as Tom Piper, and Ed Wynn as the Toymaker.

The film was based on Victor Herbert's 1903 operetta. The plot, and in some cases the music, bore little resemblance to the original, as Disney had most of the lyrics rewritten and some of the song tempos drastically changed. In 1955, Disney announced it was going to film an animated version of *Babes in Toyland*, but it was never completed.

Filming of the live-action version began March 13, 1961, and ran for three months. Walt Disney told the press that he wanted to create a film to the standard of *Wizard of Oz*. "It's like a Disney cartoon, only with live actors!" said one Disney executive.

The film begins as a stage play presented by Mother Goose and her talking goose, Sylvester. It's about Mary Mary Quite Contrary and Tom Tom, the Piper's Son, who are about to be married. It was the first time that Ray Bolger played a villain.

I received a call from the Screen Extras Guild, informing me of the dance call at Disney Studios in Burbank. Former *Mickey Mouse Club* choreographer, Tom Mahoney, recognized me at the audition and chose me for the grand opening number. I was seventeen years old.

I danced in a group of sixteen men and women, behind Mother Goose, Annette, Tommy Sands, and Ray Bolger.

I was always a high kicker and could do amazing leg-ups. I danced with a male partner in the first line of dancers and literally kicked off the first scene.

Wardrobe created a black and yellow velvet dress for me, cinched at the waist with a bunch of petticoats. I wore dark green tights underneath.

Dancing with Tommy Sands. I am second from left.

High Kicks. I am front row far left.

The opening number was truly an extrava-
ganza. Very intricate! Very Disney. Very beautiful!
Townspeople danced around Mother Goose.

Jack (who jumped over the candlestick) and some of the other high-jumping men, went to the union and demanded more money for their strenuous jumps. I think they got an extra $25.00 per jump.

It was time for Annette (Mary Quite Contrary) and Little Bo Peep (a young Ann Jillian) and her sheep to dance into the number. The sheep wasted no time, and within minutes pooped all over the set.

Everything and everyone came to a screeching halt. Studio lights turned off. Actors and techies tiptoed off the set, which was dark, quiet and smelled of sheep poop. We were paid for two days off while the crew cleaned up. Thank you, sheep family!

On another day of shooting, about a week later, we were once again dancing under the bright studio lights. Were they brighter than usual? I don't remember. But all of a sudden, the sprinkler system kicked on and poured water over the entire set, ruining most of it. We were again escorted from the studio. Repairs took an entire week, and I was paid for each day off.

Babes in Toyland

Ray Bolger's salary was hot gossip on the set. It was rumored he was making $10,000 per week. That was an enormous amount of money in 1961, and not bad, even today. We were truly honored to have the beloved Scarecrow on the set. His dancing was full of flourish and energy. And he danced it all in high-heel boots!

Pop singer and teen heartthrob Tommy Sands played the romantic male lead, Tom Piper. He sure looked good in costume... and his shiny black pompadour was amazing. I'm pretty sure that every single female on the set had a crush on him. Tommy also danced in the opening number with me. He was courting Nancy Sinatra at the time, and I remember he stopped filming several times to order dozens of roses for Nancy. I was surprised that he remembered me from the Mouseketeers.

Annette and I had a little catch-up time during the filming. Sweet, gentle and sincere, she was the same wonderful Annette I remembered.

Roustabout with Elvis Presley

In 1960, Norman Taurog directed Elvis Presley's film *G.I. Blues*, which set the tone for future films: a few girls, a few adventures, and a few songs along the way with weak plots and uninspired acting. When well made, this was an entertaining, light-hearted formula and Norman Taurog, became an old hand at it. He ensured that the films had pace, the comedy was delivered well, and the songs were well executed.

Roustabout is a 1964 American musical feature film starring Elvis Presley as a singer who takes a job working with a struggling carnival. Hal Wallis produced the film. The screenplay by Allan Weiss was nominated for a Writers Guild of America award. The film generated a best-selling soundtrack album that went #1 on the *Billboard* charts.

Some superstar actors were in the cast: Barbara Stanwyck, Jack Albertson and Leif Erickson. Raquel Welch was cast as "College Girl!"

Roustabout was the second Elvis film I auditioned for. About eighteen months earlier, I auditioned for *Harem Scarem* and got a call back. I was transitioning to live musical theater at the time and working at Melodyland Theater (see next chapter). Melodyland wouldn't let me out of my contract, so I had to turn down my first Elvis Presley harem dancing musical!

I auditioned and made the call for *Roustabout* shortly after my wedding in 1964. I was 21. I guess, I was destined to dance with Elvis Presley in another harem...in high heels, brunette wig and a veil!

The whole process took about a week to film. After we learned the dance, Elvis' stand-in came and rehearsed the song and dance. The stand-in was phenomenal. He played the guitar, and had all the Elvis moves.

Elvis walked onto the set at the exact time scheduled to shoot. Costumed! It was my first encounter with him. Tall, gorgeous and a rear-end that really moved.

Roustabout 1964. I am standing far right.

And he was as nice as he was gorgeous.

Shooting with Elvis started in the late afternoon. Up until then, we were working together in our high-heels, wigs and veils. We finished the last take at 5:45PM. I was surprised how smoothly it all transpired.

But Elvis looked at all of us and told the director: "I want to do it one more time." And when Elvis spoke to the director, everybody jumped. Somewhere in the background, I heard the producer screaming: "Oh my God, we're going into overtime."

And that's exactly why Elvis called for the re-take. We all earned an extra $25.00.

After the movie was done shooting, I was invited to a Closing Party at the studio. I was presented with a group photo of Elvis and the girls.

It was really a pleasure to work with him.

Don't Knock the Twist

Don't Knock the Twist was filmed at Columbia Studios in 1961, released in 1962. The film was directed by Oscar Rudolph and produced by Sam Katzman. It was a sequel to the 1961 film *Twist Around the Clock*.

The plot was simple and cliché-ridden. The story revolved around a group of dancers meeting in preparation for a TV variety show called (no surprise) *The Twist*. While the special was still in production stages, jealousies led to problems and a whole lot of dancing.

Filmed in black and white, the movie presented some of the greatest contemporary R&B musicians of the time. Dick Clark and "American Bandstand" was the hottest show on TV and inspired the plot. Popular songs such as "Duke of Earl" were featured in the film.

There weren't any fancy gowns. I wore a jumper, short sleeve blouse, and saddle shoes and bobby sox, with my hair in a ponytail!

It didn't take much time to learn the twist. But once learned, we spent several hours a day twisting...and still more twisting. We twisted with one leg planted on the floor. We moved and danced and twisted simultaneously. We danced within a small circle and twisted. It was all backbreaking and waist shaping. At the end of the filming, my body was toned, shapely and stronger than ever.

Doctor Doolittle (Almost!)

I was hired for the movie *Doctor Doolittle*, along with another ballerina...same height and build, for the construction of the gigantic costume of the "Push Me - Pull You." We danced on pointe. Our heads and upper bodies were very confined. Even our mouths were taped. I was very constricted and very claustrophobic. Basically, we were two white alpaca heads mounted on long necks and attached mid-torso.

But the costume was made around us.... And the producers dangled the carrot: "After the costume is done, we'll fly you to London for the filming." But it never happened because we couldn't get British working papers.

Anthony Newley was my idol! He was very dominant on the set. Very egocentric! He thought the movie was all about him.

Through my teenage years, I had been dancing in front of cameras for television and the big screen, for choreographers, directors and film editors.

The disconnected dance sequences began to feel meaningless. A five-minute dance sequence with twelve dancers was cut into many different pieces: Sometimes as many as fifty different takes were required from different camera angles. So, it took us days, even weeks to finish a routine.

We were focused on sequence steps only. There was no continuity or flow. All was dependent on how many bars were needed and what the composer wrote.

After a few years in front of the cameras, I yearned to dance a routine from beginning to end: a complete performance, in front of a live audience.

As I entered my twenties, I wanted to feel audience response. It was time for something different. But first...

CHAPTER EIGHT

I Get Married

Upon reflection, my life as it is today, really started with my husband Roy.

Roy

The person I love and depend upon most in my life is my husband, Roy. We've been blessed with two incredible children, Shahna and Joshua, our son-in-law, Jeremy, and grandson, Jonah.

Intertwining careers have kept us stimulated and creative for the last 50+ years. And lots of passion, on stage and off!

In 1963, I was 20 and a student at UCLA, enrolled in a class called Musical Theater Workshop. I took the class because had heard great things about the teacher, Bob Mesrobian. Roy was his teaching assistant and ran most of the practical work done in class.

On the first day of class, Roy went to each student and asked their name. "What's your name?" he asked me. For some reason, I got belligerent and roared back: "What's *your* name?" And that was the beginning of a friendship, partnership and love affair going into its sixth decade.

During the semester, we did a production of *Fiorello*, the 1959 hit musical about the colorful mayor of 1930's New York City. I was cast as Dora, opposite Roy who played Floyd the Cop. I sang my first love song to Roy, "I Love a Cop." Roy had trouble remembering his lines when I was done with the song. I knew I had gotten his attention.

In addition to my classwork at UCLA, I kept up with auditions for live theater and film work. I was called for a film audition at MGM. I don't remember the name of the film, but they were looking for a Mitzi Gaynor-type. I read for the part and was called back for a second reading. The director asked me to bring a male actor to read the scene with me. I asked Roy and he agreed.

Knowing they were looking for a cute and glamorous debutant, I dressed for the part: high heels, grown-up-sexy-polka-dot dress, matching coat, and my hair done up in a French Twist.

I don't remember if we exchanged words before the reading, but Roy kept looking at me and smiling. We read the scene for the director, while staring deeply into each other's eyes. And Roy kept smiling.

That MGM moment was the beginning of our romance. A truly magical moment...so alive and exciting...and very real for both of us.

Our first date after the reading was strange. I think Roy was expecting that same curvaceous girl in the tight, sexy polka dot dress. Instead, I dressed like a true college coed in bobby sox and all. I thought that's what he wanted and who he expected me to be. Not quite.

We went to a concert at UCLA, then Roy drove us to the beach. We sat in the front seat of his car and talked. It was a bit awkward, and then I looked deep into his eyes and sang Barbra Streisand's newest hit song "My Coloring Book." I belted it out. I hit the final crescendo and immediately Roy turned the key in the ignition and drove me home! He walked Miss Bobby Sox to the door and said, "I'll see you around."

Without even thinking, I said, "When?"

"What do you mean 'when?'" he asked.

"I mean... When?!" I replied.

Roy managed to squeak out "Saturday!" and jumped into his car before I had a chance to seal it with a kiss.

Roy loves retelling this story: when he got home, his mother asked, "How did it go?"

"It was the worst date I ever had," he told his mother.

"Well, chalk it up to experience. At least you'll never have to go out with her again," his mother replied.

"I'll know better next week," he told her.

"What does that mean?" she asked.

After all these years, Roy can finally smile when he says, "She tricked me into inviting her out again!"

A college education didn't interrupt my career, but nobody could keep up with my street smarts... not even Roy!

We set a wedding date of September 13, 1964.

We invited Walt Disney to the wedding. He didn't attend, but sent a nice note

On our wedding night we stayed at the Beverly Rodeo Hotel. Roy's parents were staying two floors below us.

We got on the elevator, rode down two floors. I knocked on the door of his parent's room. "What do we do next?" I asked. They were absolutely hysterical.

We were both so naïve. We didn't know anything

about each other. Not about traveling. It was pretty primitive. It's amazing we survived any of it. But we did survive, and we learned and loved and mastered it all!

CHAPTER NINE

Me, on Stage for the First Time

My live performance career began in 1949. I auditioned for a play called *Monday's Heroes*, directed by Morris Carnovsky at the Young Actor's Lab on Sunset Strip.

Morris Carnovsky was an acting legend. He got his start in the Yiddish Theater and was a founder of the Group Theater in New York in 1931. His acting career on Broadway and in films thrived until the early 1950s when Carnovsky was called before the House Un-American Activities Committee, admitted he had been a member of the Communist Party, and was blacklisted, which I met him.

I do remember a lot of big-time stars and movie people came to see the show. And I loved acting on stage.

Most of my teenage years were spent in television

)AILY NEWS, LOS ANGELES— SATURDAY, DEC. 17, 1949 . . 23

EILEEN DIAMOND in "Monday's Heroes," Actors Lab production showing weekends only at the Lab Workshop theater.

★ Film rev

studios and movie sound stages, performing bits and pieces of song and dance. In my late teens, I realized that musical theater would enable me to utilize all my talents. Straight through, from Act-One, Scene-One to the final curtain.

I saw "West Side Story" on Broadway when it opened in 1957. That performance changed my life. I wanted to be one of those dancers, singers and actors. I knew I could do it.

The Beginning

The El Capitan Theater on Hollywood Boulevard in 1958 is where I made my musical theater debut in *Most Happy Fella*. I was fifteen and already a veteran of film and TV dance.

I was cast as 'Young Girl Dancer!' I sang and danced in the chorus and loved every single minute of the performance, from beginning to end. Hallelujah.

Live musical theater was more fulfilling than any other work I had done so far. Working straight through, alongside choreographers and directors to final curtain, was a whole new experience for me. I watched the entire process bloom into a glorious two and a half-hour production.

I was always the strongest dancer and led the other dancers. How did I achieve such a feat? Focus is still my life's mantra. Focus on what you are doing and enjoy yourself while doing it. An agent saw me during the auditions, and signed me. It was necessary, and became mandatory for me to become a member of Actor's Equity. (This is the union that sets rules for the payment and working conditions for actors.)

Many times, the producers and directors talked directly with theatrical agents before auditions began. Don Wortman was my theatrical agent at the Ashley Famous Agency. He worked on musical shows across the country. Eventually, he had a successful career of his own as a casting director.

After a while, my resume included many different shows, and enabled me to repeat roles with different companies. Dancing auditions became a matter of 'Bring your dance shoes.' And "bring your union card!"

In the beginning of my career, I learned all the steps. Eventually "Young Girl Dancer" stepped in front of the chorus and began playing speaking and singing roles.

The biggest adjustment for me was learning lines. So much to memorize! No familiar techniques to rely on. I spoke too fast. I had to slow down and understand what I was saying and that took some time to master. Live musical theater is truly an art form of its own. I don't ever remember being emotional while working. Emotions and nerves were reserved for auditions.

Performing for a live audience was much more compelling than my previous TV and film work. The rehearsal process started with the director, stage manager and choreographer. The choreographer made sure all the dances were learned and correctly executed during the rehearsals. When the show was up and running, the stage manager watched each performance and reported to the choreographer any incidents where dancers either didn't follow or improvised on their own.

The stage manager took copious notes on blocking and staging. We were never allowed to change any moves. If we did, the stage-manager wrote a note to the choreographer.

I remember working with a young guy who constantly goofed around. One day, he stepped out of line during rehearsal, made some suggestions of his own and was instantly fired.

Innately, you should have enough talent to pick

up all the details of the routine. If you didn't get the underlying motivation from the director, you had to create it yourself.

I learned the process by watching and listening. I listened to recordings. Listened to what the other actors, directors and choreographers were saying. Most importantly, I listened to other people doing scenes with me. That's where my cues came from. I had to memorize my lines and learn lines from all the other actors on stage with me.

In the 60s, the venues were theaters-in-the round and were tech savvy. Microphones were suspended from the upper grids above the stage. Some of the lead performers wore lapel mics, mics in their hair or transmitter mics with fanny packs. (A girl I worked with, ran to the bathroom between scenes but the sound engineer forgot to turn off her mic and the entire audience heard the toilet flush!)

I was always the loudest female singer on stage. I knew how to 'belt' it out and make my voice fill the theater.

Performance workdays (or nights) started in the dressing rooms. We put on our own make-up and costumes. There was a wardrobe mistress available for quick changes. Because the performance was ongoing, actors and dancers had to run off stage and quickly dress for the next scene.

Gone were the days of the dressers and make-up people on TV and movies sets. I learned that live stage work was more homegrown and hands-on. I had to depend solely on myself for costume changes and makeup.

CHAPTER TEN

Live Musical Theatre

My life has always revolved around performance: as a theatrical agent, as a choreographer, director and writer, and of course, as a singer and dancer. One thing led to another, so this chapter is about my experience in musical theater.

Melodyland

My first experience as part of a repertory company (an established theatrical group that stages shows as a regular ensemble but with rotating stars) was at Melodyland Theater. Ironically, the theater was located in Anaheim, across Harbor Boulevard from Disneyland. Melodyland opened in 1963. The 3200-seat theater in the round offered Broadway musicals, concerts by popular performers and even ice shows. Now, the building is a church.

Although I was only there for six months, it was truly a 'season!' We did 10 shows over six months. We rehearsed during the day and performed at night, seven days a week, evening performances and matinees.

Irving Berlin's *Annie Get Your Gun* was the first show mounted at Melodyland. I danced in the show. Betty Hutton starred as Annie and Harve Presnell played Frank Butler.

Harve starred in the movie *The Unsinkable Molly Brown*, opposite Debbie Reynolds. He was indeed, eye-candy! But he was also one of the nicest men I ever worked with. He always took all the dancers out to eat and then back to his house for some swimming.

Music Man at Melodyland.

The season continued with *Bye Bye Birdie*, in which I played 'Sad Girl' and danced with George Gobel to "Put on a Happy Face." I was in *Guys and Dolls* starring Betty Grable. We did *The Unsinkable Molly Brown*, with Jane Powell, and *Fire Fly* with Anna Maria Alberghetti.

No stranger to Meredith Wilson's *The Music Man*, I also played in a production at Melodyland.

The Sacramento Music Circus

I started at The Sacramento Music Circus in the summer of 1964. It was a great experience for me. I truly learned my trade there. In summer stock, we had to learn a complete show in one week's time. I started there in the summer of 1964, when Roy was the Assistant Conductor.

The Music Circus was housed in an enormous canvas tent. We worked through the heat of the day inside that tent. I took a lot of salt pills to keep from passing out. We had five hours of rehearsal during the day and three hours of performance each night. Subsequently, the tent was torn down and replaced by a concrete, state-of-the-art, air-conditioned theater.

That was my life and I LOVED working with professionals from Broadway and Hollywood. In time, I started doing featured roles.

Stop the World I Want to Get Off opened on Broadway in 1962, with music, lyrics and book by Leslie Bricusse and Anthony Newley. I had a featured role as one of the daughters., my most challenging part to date. I was quite excited over this because the show was all new to me. This was the source of Newley's song, "What Kind of Fool Am I?"

The lead, Kenny Nelson was Anthony Newley's understudy in the show and created "The Boy" in the original production of *The Fantastick*s. Milton Lyons co-directed the show.

Paint Your Wagon followed, starring the great Larry Kert, who was Tony in the original Broadway production of *West Side Story*. I saw him perform the role at the Winter Garden Theatre in New York in 1958. He was my first Broadway heartthrob and now we were dancing and singing together on stage! Working alongside him was a major joy

I also sang and danced in Rodgers and Hammerstein's *Flower Drum Song* and Cole Porter's *Kiss Me Kate*.

My most outstanding memory of the Sacramento Music Circus

Stop the World I Want to Get Off.

was the entire company on stage in *She Loves Me*. An overhead trapdoor above center stage was packed with artificial snow. During the song, the trapdoor was supposed to open. But that night, it jammed and the artificial snow caught on fire.

Audience, performers and techies got out of there in a hurry, as the maintenance crew rushed in. The fire was declared "out." The seats and stage were scrubbed clean. Everybody returned to their seats. The actors took their places on stage, the musicians were in the pit, and the show resumed! It was amazing. "The show must go on!" And it did.

Out West

At the end of the summer season of the Sacramento Music Circus, Roy and I were invited to continue for the fall season in Fresno, but we had made our wedding plans by this time.

Yellowstone

Roy returned to UCLA to finish up his Bachelor's Degree in Music and I studied Existentialism and Italian on extension. At the end of the year when Roy had earned his degree, Cum Laude I might add, we were invited to Montana, of all places, to take over a barn theatre in West Yellowstone. You could call the experience "Cowboy Rustic."

Every night we rode through town on an authentic old stagecoach pulled by two very decrepit and unwilling horses. We barged into crowded restaurants every night, sang a song or two, and invited everyone to see the show.

Most of the entertainment was old vaudeville routines called "olio's,'" some of which we had written ourselves. We had roll drops, which changed with each scene to identify different locations.

Everything was light musical comedy. For instance: A girl entered the stage, dressed in a formal gown and belted out a classical operatic aria. The audience applauded dutifully. She curtsied, thanked the audience, lifted her long gown revealing roller-skates and skated off the stage. I did a Marilyn Monroe skit with my voluptuous puckered lips and not very much of anything else voluptuous, repeating a breathy "Hello" several times and finally yelled out "Oh Hell!" and exited.

Yellowstone was my introduction to roughing it. A late-night bathroom break meant walking to the theatre in the dead of night, past rows of garbage cans and lots of bears chowing down. The first time I ran into a bear, literally, I screamed and Roy came running. He saw what I saw, and we both backed up slowly, knowing that if we ran, the bears would mistake us for lunch. We tiptoed back to our rustic cabin, with no electricity, no running water and no bathrooms. We cooked dinner, such as it was, on a hot plate.

"Hot Potting" was our favorite late-night activity. Hot Pots are natural pools of boiling water situated near geysers. Sneaking into and skinny-dipping in the safe ones was a welcome relief from the rigors of rehearsing all day and performing all night. One night, a Park Ranger appeared at the edge of the pool we were about to enter. We were pleasantly surprised, when instead of arresting us, he directed us to a different pool suggesting that the one we were going to use would fry us!

Bountiful, Utah

At the end of the season, Roy was hired as the conductor at a brand-new 3,500 seat, state-of-the-art theatre-in-the round called the Valley Music Hall. He was understandably panicked, because it was his first professional job as a conductor with full orchestra pit and well-known musical stars.

One of the company members had to leave, unexpectedly and Roy suggested me as a replacement. The director and choreographer begrudgingly agreed to audition me, thinking that Roy was just trying to give his wife a chance. I can still see their expressions when they saw an experienced actor and triple-threat singer-dancer strutting her stuff in front of them. When they learned that I had done summer stock, television and films, they couldn't wait to cast me in a series of leading roles. They never expected a Disney Mouseketeer to be lighting up their stage.

Roy was a hero, and I was thrilled to be moving on to lead roles. It was just another in a succession of professional jobs that started with the Mouseketeers nearly ten years earlier. Finally, I had hit my stride. I realized that work in live musical theatre was my real passion.

The Houston Music Theatre

Built in 1965, The Houston Music Theatre in the Houston suburb of Sharpstown was a 2,850-seat arena built in the round. Bob Hope was one of the original investors.

I was one of the first members of the repertory company. I was able to play featured roles on a regular basis.

In the Rogers and Hart classic musical *Pal Joey* I played Gladys Bumps. Bobby Van starred. Working with him was awesome. In fact, I knew his fiancée Elaine Joyce (we called her Bubbles) as we danced together in Balanchine's *Nutcracker Suite*. (see photo at page 22) A nice Jewish girl, and a teeny-weeny pug nose! During one rehearsal he said, "You remind me of Elaine!"

Bobby, Roy and I went out for a late supper after the show one night. Roy and I both wore similar glasses and after that night and for the rest of the time we knew him, he always called us "Mr. & Mrs. Glasses."

Oklahoma! was Rodgers and Hammerstein's first collaboration and a popular favorite. I played two roles: Dancing Laurie and Giggling Gertie. The roles were nice, but the best part was that I got to do them with John Raitt.

John Raitt was best known for his Broadway starring roles in the musicals *Carousel, Oklahoma!* and *The Pajama Game.* In *Oklahoma,* Giggling Gertie was the girl who showed off her wedding ring to the crowd and giggled. I had the best giggle-snorting in the world, prolonged and very contagious. Within seconds I could get the whole audience laughing and applauding.

I started running up the aisles giggling my head off, with a phenomenal cackle typically rewarded with spontaneous applause. John Raitt was a real gentleman, and he'd just stand on stage waiting for the laughter to die down before speaking his next lines. Now that's a generous leading man. His silence prompted the audience's applause.

The ultimate compliment was that, at the end of the run, John Raitt told me I was the best Giggling Gertie he had ever heard!

I played Claudine in Cole Porter's sassy *Can-Can.* The story concerns the showgirls of the Montmartre dance halls during the 1890s. The production starred Anne Miller and John Cullum.

Howard Keel starred in *Pajama Game.* I played Gladys Hotchkiss and danced the part that Carol Haney danced in the Broadway show. (A bit of Broadway trivia, one night, Carol Haney injured herself and her young understudy, Shirley MacLaine went on, and the rest is showbiz history).

Howard Keel, with his macho good looks and rich bass-baritone voice, had starred in some of the

With Alan Jenkins in *Pal Joey*.

most famous MGM musicals ever made. I remember *The Pajama Game* most of all. He took me aside one day and told me: "Never go to bed in the middle of an argument!" Good advice from a three-times married bass baritone.

Wild Cat opened on Broadway in 1960, with music and lyrics by Cy Coleman and Carolyn Leigh, with Lucille Ball in the lead. Martha Raye took over the lead at the Houston Music Theatre, and I played her younger sister, Janie.

At the time, Martha was a major American star, with her own prime-time musical variety TV show, movie roles and nightclub and concert performances. Martha and I stood side-by-side center stage and belted out the show's hit song, "Hey, Look Me Over!"

Take Me Along, the musical version of a play by Eugene O'Neil, opened on Broadway 1959. I performed this show on several different occasions and played opposite to Ron de Salvo.

With Neil Nixon in *The Pajama Game*.

Take Me Along at the Houston Music Theatre.

Before becoming a Beverly Hills real estate mogul, Ron was a leading man in the musical theater circuit. We were the Lunt and Fontaine of Summer Stock Theater. We also played opposite each other in *Wild Cat* and *Pajama Game*. We still remain close after all these years.

I have a lot of memories of Houston aside from the roles I played. During a performance of *Oklahoma!* we were deluged with pouring rain. The lights went out and water started flooding the theater, stage and audience. I remember a cellist crawled out of the pit with cello in hand, held high above his head.

I also remember a publicity photo shoot at NASA. We met all the astronauts, were presented with autographed photos, viewed all the spaceships up close and personal and visited the launch pad.

Roy and I also had the pleasure of becoming friends with Lawrence Marcus. At the time, Lawrence was running the Houston branch of the world-famous department store Neiman Marcus. Lawrence, known as "Lawry," was one of the four sons of founder, Herbert Marcus.

At NASA in Houston: I am first row, far right.

Lawry came to many of our performances. He invited us out to dinner after the shows and began hosting lavish parties for the cast at his home.

One particular party at the Marcus house stands out in my mind. Lawrence Marcus had a very serious art collection. Lots of Ben Shahn, my favorite artist. There was a Modigliani painting leaning against the wall in the middle of the living room. On the coffee table, was a bronze maquette of a hand created by Rodin. Priceless? You bet. The hand was just resting on the coffee table.

Two days later, the entire cast and crew were force-fully invited back to the Marcus home. The Rodin hand was missing. Martha Raye reached into her purse and put the Rodin hand back on the table. "I was a little drunk," she apologized to Lawrence Marcus. "I just put it into my purse without thinking."

Goodspeed Opera House

After Houston, we moved to the now-legendary Goodspeed Opera House in Connecticut where I became the resident ingénue and Roy conducted the orchestra and later became associate producer. Years earlier, the theatre premiered *Man of La Mancha* and sent it directly to Broadway. Later on, Goodspeed secured its reputation by launching an unknown show called "Annie," which quickly moved to Broadway. The Goodspeed continues to have a financial participation.

I did *Peter Pan*, (music by Jules Styne, Mark Charlap and Trude Ritman, lyrics by Betty Comden, Adolph Green and Carolyn Leigh) the very first winter production at the Salt Lake City Music Hall, playing Mrs. Darling opposite Victor Buono as Mr. Darling/Captain Hook. I sang "Tender Shepherd." Tony Geary, later to become Luke Spencer in *General Hospital*, was in the show. Luke crawled across the stage in an alligator suit.

I followed up with the lead in *The Boyfriend*, and went on to do the lead in the premiere of a new musical, *Tom Piper*.

I played the lead, Molly, in George Gershwin's *Girl Crazy*. The title was changed to "Crazy for You" which

Mrs. Darling in *Peter Pan* at the Salt Lake City Music Hall.

later moved to Broadway and won the Tony Award for Best New Musical and the Laurence Olivier Award for Best Musical Revival in 1992.

By the summer of 1970, I was married and mother of one-year-old Shahna. I was still touring the live musical theater circuit, traveling with baby and her nanny.

Roy was traveling around the country conducting for Johnny Mathis and he came to the Goodspeed to surprise me while I was doing *Girl Crazy*. Roy was standing in the wings. At the end of the show, I ran off stage and straight into his arms. I was dripping wet and exhausted. I started crying, "Why would anyone do this?" I asked. "I have a daughter and I want to be a mother. I don't want to perform any more!"

CHAPTER ELEVEN

Motherhood: Entrances and Exits in My Life

It was 1970. There I was, lying in bed shaking all over. I had just hung up the phone. Roy had just opened in Chicago conducting for Johnny Mathis. "I'll call you after I speak with the doctor."

I called my doctor and he asked if I had any contractions. I said, "Yes, they are about 3 minutes apart." He instructed me to go the hospital at once and he would meet me there.

I called Roy back in Chicago and told him I'm going to the hospital and he should begin to get ready to call his replacement. The doctor had told me in advance there was no need for my husband to rush. I'd probably be in labor for 10 hours or so.

We had it all arranged. My girlfriend, Diane Pershing, would pick me up to go to the hospital and her husband, D'arneill, also a conductor, would go to Chicago to replace Roy, while he flew to Los Angeles.

This was, of course, 3 in the morning. Diane picked me up. I was in shock and didn't want to go. I thought it was too soon, especially since Roy was not there. I tried to prolong it as long as possible. Diane threw me bodily into the car. I hadn't even packed my suitcase yet. So off we went for the 10-minute drive to the hospital. I wasn't looking forward to the enema which everyone said I had to have. I was shaking all over with an anxiety attack.

I was sitting in a wheelchair at the hospital's emergency entrance registering and filling out forms for what seemed like forever when I finally told the nurse that my water broke an hour ago! She lunged at the wheelchair without another word and drove me upstairs.

I was placed in the Labor Room and the head nurse came in to examine me. I was already 8 centimeters dilated and did not need an enema; my doctor was on his way to the room. My water turned out to be only half broken at the top and there was more fluid hanging in the bottom of the sac. The doctor examined me internally. He said, "This won't hurt," and came at me with what looked like a long sword. The rest of my water broke and my doctor told me he was going to have a cup of coffee. I yelled, "Don't go, the baby is coming!" I felt an enormous pressure and nearly passed out cold.

The next thing, they were wheeling me into the delivery room and within seconds I saw Shahna being born. First her little head and hand. Then my doctor said, "It's got to be a girl because her hand is the first things out." She had long black hair and was born within 3 hours. I was in good health and my husband was not there.

My father had gone to pick Roy up at the airport and already told him it was a girl. Roy had just come from seeing the baby and the first thing he said to me was that I had given birth to Attila the Hun!

All I could do was stare out the window. Across the street was the Disney Studio. My life flashed in front of me and I wished I was back on the lot singing and dancing with all my heart. I didn't care if I was being told what to do. I was a child there and didn't have to be grown up and have a child of my own. I was begging for someone to tell me what to do.

In a few moments, my baby was in my arms for the first time. I would nurse her and feel for the first time, someone really depending on me to be nurtured and loved and fed. All the things a mom does for her child. I was nursing her and feeling wanted for the first time. She needed me and I didn't feel she was a crutch for me, or a cop-out.

We all need to be loved and have our egos fed. We must leave ourselves open to the world and not close ourselves off. We must live our lives and receive all the information with open arms. There is a world out there. Don't limit yourself to your own confines. Don't be afraid of men; we are their equals, if not more. They are unable to experience the true feeling of reproducing and giving birth to another identity.

Nine months prior to all this excitement, Roy and I had decided it was time to start a family. A few weeks later, Roy and I were having dinner with my sister, Harriet and her husband at our favorite restaurant, The Smoke House, in the San Fernando Valley.

The place was always crowded, but on this particular night (*Why was this night different from all others?*) the whole place was abuzz. A famous corporate handwriting analyst was drawing attention, going from table to table, scrutinizing signatures and making predictions.

When he arrived at our table, all four of us signed napkins and handed them over. He stared long and hard at my signature. Then looked me directly in the eye:

"Are you married?" he asked.

He turned his gaze on Roy: "Is this your husband?"

Everybody at the table nodded.

"You're pregnant!" he announced. "I can see the pregnancy in your signature."

A few days later, I saw my doctor, took a pregnancy test and it was affirmed: POSITIVE!

"Benjamin or Joshua!" we both proclaimed. Boy's names were easy. No doubts. But girl's names were a challenge. We referred to HER as Baby Girl Rogosin.

Early on in the pregnancy, I traveled to New York with Roy for business and pleasure when Roy was conducting for Johnny Mathis. Our daytime hours were devoted to Museums and art exhibitions throughout the city. We found our way to an exhibition of Ben Shahn.

We were both overwhelmed with one particular lithograph, "Flowering Brushes." Black and white, except for an explosion of colorful flowers: A young man holding a bouquet of wild flowers blooming out of a handful of color saturated paint brushes.

At the top of the lithograph was a writing by Hillel: "If I am not for myself, who will be for me? If I am for myself alone, what am I? If not now, when?"

Roy and I fell in love with Ben Shahn at that moment. We purchased the lithograph. Our eyes locked together, we both lowered our heads and focused on my "baby-bump" and proclaimed: "Baby Girl Rogosin is now Shahna!"

As I mentioned, I had returned to the Goodspeed Opera House in Connecticut to get back to my life on the stage, but now something was definitely different. My only vocational aspiration after "Girl Crazy" was to be a world-class mom. I spent the next seven years loving and nurturing Shahna and her brother, Joshua,

My son, Joshua Hillel Rogosin was born in 1975 at St. Joseph's Hospital, where Shahna was born. Again, I found myself looking across the street at the Disney Studio thinking of younger and simpler days spent singing and dancing.

Josh's musical talents were obvious at a very early age. He loved to sing and he always sang on key. Music was his passion. His voice matured into a glorious baritone-tenor.

Renowned photographer and composer Cy Miller
snapped the photo of Shahna and me.

One day Roy put his conducting baton into Josh's baby hand and counted out beats and measures. Josh followed along naturally. Josh got his musical talents from Roy and me. He heard the music in his head all the time and started writing and performing his own original songs with his guitar even before he was a teenager.

When he was five, Joshua proved himself to have real, natural talent with a beautiful singing voice, and like his mom, wanted to perform. A friend who was a manager for child performers sent me to the Eileen Farrell Agency, strictly a children's agency.

After the kids were in school and self-sufficient, I got the creative itch once again. I had years of experience on stage, and now it was time to start working behind the scenes.

I volunteered my past experience to Eileen and offered to assist her. I had been working in the business since I was six years old. I knew she had to find kids who were talented, dedicated, and would persevere, and at the same time, be able to take rejection. I worked with many gifted young people, teaching them how to audition and prepare for interviews.

My career as casting director and agent started booming with Eileen Farrell. I found work for hundreds of kids. Eileen nicknamed me "Booker T," for Booking Talent. I later went on to the Sutton Barth and Venari Agency where I worked as an assistant commercial agent.

After our return from Europe the Rogosin family moved to Palm Springs for a few years in the early 1980s. I began teaching acting and music classes to the local kids.

Fast-forward to a quick decade later: we moved back East. I found myself working as a casting director once again, with Roy in our educational and theatrical endeavors at the Seacoast Repertory Theater in Portsmouth, NH and the Ogunquit Playhouse in Maine.

A Passing

When I was nine months pregnant with Joshua, my sister Harriet was hit and killed by a car while she was crossing Pacific Coast Highway. She was 36. What do you say? What are my thoughts? She is gone and I am here. I carry on. My mom and dad go on. But her short life is at an end. She lived her 36 years and the chapter is closed for her. She won't have a chance to become older.

Oh God, why do these things have to happen? How could I have prevented it? You see, now I'm trying to play God. Oh, the pain and anguish. Was she in pain? Did she feel anything I had a vision of her saying "It's going to be all right. I'm really fine. Don't worry about me."

A few weeks before she died, Harriet put her arms around me and told me she loved me. It was the first time in her 36 years that she told me she loved me. What a rude awakening not to have her there anymore just when we were getting to love one another. Why do we do these things to ourselves? Why do we make things so complicated? Thank God it happened at all between us before her death. I love you Roy with all my heart and body. I love you, Mom and Dad. I love you Harriet forever.

At the funeral, my father threw himself on the casket and cried. At that moment, I remember wishing that it was me in the casket, receiving my father's love.

I love you Shahna, my first-born. Oh, if Harriet could have seen Joshua. She would never have believed that I would have a boy. The baby was about to take his first breath while my sister took her last.

Suddenly, I'm a parent again to my sister's sixteen-year-old daughter, Teri Lynn. I am appointed guardian and she is also living in our household. Right now, everything seems so overwhelming, too much for anyone to handle. But we do, don't we? We go on. The fear of dying doesn't seem so big when it is at hand. It takes the young as well as the old. There is no warning. Is there such a thing as fate? Everything up to Harriet's death seemed to be choreographed. I keep waking up and saying, "Isn't it all a bad dream?" Pinch me and tell me it didn't happen. Somehow, I'm not afraid anymore. I have a calm about me.

Roy's mom was talking once about the fear of death. I talked about it very casually with her. You are born innocent and the older you are; more fears develop with the ensuing knowledge of life. Isn't that bizarre? What is the difference between fear of flight and fear of failing or fear of death? It all keeps you from living, doesn't it?

Shahna is now 50. She is a pediatric psychiatrist, married to Jeremy, a rheumatologist and they are the proud parents of our beloved grandson, Jonah.

Josh is now a preeminent sound engineer and technical director at NPR, and a producer, recording their flagship podcast, "Tiny Desk Concerts." The host, Bob Boilen, became his champion. Josh has traveled the world and captured music and sound.

Roy and I always believed that raising the

With Josh at our North Hollywood home.

kids was a creative process. We tried to open their minds to the world and its endless possibilities. And we showed them by example and by including them in our adventures before they could walk.

Innocents Abroad

When he was music supervisor at Universal Studios, Roy called from work and said he was bringing someone home for dinner: Academy Award-winning French composer Michel Legrand, who had just finished a recording session with Roy for his next picture. "Let's go to a restaurant," I shouted into the phone. "I'm not cooking for Michel Legrand." Roy arrived later with Michel, whom he brought home despite my unmistakable warning.

I can't remember what I cooked, but the two of them seemed to enjoy it, while I tried not to throw up. We were sitting at the table having dessert, when Michel leaned back in his chair and asked, "So, Eileen... how

Michel Legrand and Roy in Paris.

do you feel about moving to Paris?" There was a long silence, and the next thing I remember was arriving in Paris seven weeks later with two children, ages one and six, and all our portable worldly possessions. No turning back now.

Paris is where I began writing my Mouseketeers Memoir and also working with my friend, Ann Gratton, on a movie script. My first attempt at writing. Paris was four years of enlightenment, art, friendship, dancing and museums, which I hope to expound upon in a future book. We returned to the United States four years later on the Queen Elizabeth II, with 17 pieces of luggage and memories beyond belief.

The Rogosin family with "Opus."

CHAPTER TWELVE

Opening Night

In 1980, Roy was producing his first musical in London, a stage version of Michel Legrand's *Umbrellas of Cherbourg*.

I had just had a bout with bronchitis and was nursing a bad cough with all sorts of remedies and antibiotics. While taxiing down the runway on the Laker Skytrain on the flight to London, I think I managed to infect everyone with whatever was ailing me.

I was traveling with Roy's parents, his brother, and his brother's wife. We were to be gone for 13 days. Roy rented us a mews for our stay in London. A mews was a row house originally used as a stable. Now, however, it is a very desirable flat.

We were still very excited in spite of all our illnesses. Roy was to meet us at Victoria Station in London after we took the train from Gatwick Airport. He didn't let us down, for there was a beautiful English Daimler Limousine. We were elated to see one another. Roy had arrived in London a month earlier to ready the production oversee the rehearsal schedule. The rainy weather didn't dampen our reunion.

We drove down a narrow, winding cobblestone street before arriving at our mews. It looked as if it were right out of a Dickens novel. We were in the best section of town, Belgravia and Knightsbridge, right around the corner from Harrods. We were exhausted, but who cared? This was going to be a once-in-a-lifetime experience.

Our flat was four stories high. You entered on the ground floor where there was just a staircase that looked as if it were going straight up vertically for two flights. Once you made it to the first landing, it didn't seem so horrible.

Our twenty pieces of luggage didn't help the situation. The first landing consisted of a bedroom for Roy's parents, and a bathroom, and a kitchen with a dumb-waiter. The second floor had a dining room with no light and a huge living room the size of a bowling alley, with a bar and desk and a couple of sofas and chairs. The top floor had, of all things, a sauna with a toilet and tub and a small bedroom for Roy's brother and his wife. It was enchanting. I just knew chimney sweeps would be dropping in at any moment.

Upon our arrival we changed our clothes and went immediately around the corner to a little restaurant where we enjoyed our first meal in London. The whole family was together for the first time in many months. We finally began to relax after our long journey. We had been awake the entire plane trip because, unfortunately, we were seated right next to the United States Rugby Team. And to our dismay, they returned on the same flight with us thirteen days later. What a horrible coincidence! We managed to survive in spite of them but were exhausted and drained, and our trip had just begun.

We all looked like the cat dragged us in when we got back to the flat. Roy's parents barely made it up the first flight while leaving a trail of coughs behind them. My father-in-law had major surgery two months prior to our leaving Los Angeles, and I was the one who talked him into coming to London. So, I felt responsible for his condition, even though, he was putting up a good front.

Soon, everything started falling into place. We were breaking in the flat. Or should I say the flat was breaking us in! The sauna was a getaway for the men. Late at night, after rehearsal, all the men would climb in and relax. I'm glad at least something worked in this flat. The hot water was the bane of everyone's existence. It never worked. After one person took a bath, that was it for the whole day! I did a lot of sponging off.

We were paying over $1000 a week for the flat. We split it 3 ways so it came out a lot cheaper than a hotel. So, I guess we were willing to put up with some of its idiosyncrasies. It is very different from America where we are accustomed to everything working properly. Well, it just isn't that way in Europe.

My days and nights consisted of going to watch rehearsals, shopping at Harrods and touring Sloane Street, walking everywhere, and generally exhausting myself. All of our respective colds and flu seemed to hang on and got even worse. We just couldn't shake them off with all of this running around we were doing.

Unfortunately, Roy's mom was starting to look really unwell so we telephoned the theater's doctor on call and he arrived at midnight. That is one thing that would never happen in America. The doctor examined us all and put us back on antibiotics and cough medicines. That night we went to sleep in a cacophony of coughing.

Back at the theater, the rehearsals were not going well. The director had the actors moving around large Plexiglas panels as part of the scenery. They were on rollers and were nearly impossible to move without making a lot of noise. Sometimes the effect worked and other times they just sat there getting in the way of the actors. But the director insisted on using them.

I was ill and it wasn't just from my coughing. But I was just one of the producer's wives, so they were not listening to me. One of the comments I overheard at a trial performance from the audience was that it looked like the actors were singing through a refrigerator.

Two days before opening, some dear friends from Los Angeles showed great class and arrived at our flat and surprised us. We were overcome and appreciative of their support. Within the next two days, four more arrived at our doorstep. Most of them stayed with other friends in London or in hotels. Yet another friend, Richard Merrill and his new wife Aida, flew in from San Francisco and stayed with us and slept on yoga mats on the floor of our overcrowded mews.

Richard was largely responsible for raising much of the needed monies to capitalize the show from his colleagues in Silicon Valley. We now had a full house of friends and family, with many others scattered about the city.

Amidst all this excitement, Roy was eating in a pub with our friends the day before opening, and his man-bag was stolen. It contained his work papers, passport, credit cards, travelers' checks, money and his favorite Dupont pens which he had collected over the past three years. Roy was devastated. He spent most of the day at Scotland Yard while I spent the rest of the day calling all the credit card companies to cancel the cards. Still, the show must go on.

The following morning was the beginning of an exciting day for all of us. It was opening night. I went over to Harrods for a complete makeover including a massage, steam, shower (Thank God) hair, and nails, - the works!

If I may say so myself, I was looking quite lovely for the event. All of our outfits were sent to the cleaners in the morning. They were picked up and delivered to us in time for the opening. I was wearing a long gown and Roy had on his tuxedo and silk shirt and bow tie. We were all dressed to the hilt and looked extremely chic.

The tension and excitement were mounting. We were feeling so much support from all our friends and family. There was so much love all around us. The limos were to arrive at six for the seven o'clock opening curtain. Just as we were leaving the flat, the phone rang and Roy's dad answered it.

It was the police chief from Scotland Yard asking if Roy's dad was the Rogosin "whose pouch was pinched at Piccadilly?"

Of course, we hadn't bothered telling Roy's mom and dad about the theft because we didn't want to worry them. They seemed to have enough to handle with them both being sick. We didn't want them any more upset. So, we had to fess up in the limousine on the way to the theater.

There must have been at least twenty people in our party. We all felt like the beautiful people at the Ascot Gavotte.

Roy and I sat front row balcony. My heart was pounding along with the overture. Thank God, the violins were playing together and in tune. The night went swimmingly well and the audience stood and yelled bravos for what seemed a very long time. I felt a great weight lifted off my shoulders, as if by magic. Was it all over or was this just the beginning?

There was a reception after the show, and then all of us went back to the flat to await the results of the reviews. The night seemed never-ending; it was a blur from then on. I only remember Richard, our investor friend, reading the reviews in the kitchen the next morning and saying "Oh my God! Oy Vey! And "No! No!"

Here are some of the reviewers' well-chosen words: "I can't ever remember sitting through an evening of sentimental bosh." "Sitting through the Umbrellas of Cherbourg at the Phoenix is like surviving a hailstorm of marshmallows." "Every now and then the theatre takes a determined step backwards." "What we have is an immensely sentimental story told in prose lines set to music that plods along in a heavy-footed common time most of the evening." "It's a grossly incompetent piece of story-telling." "They raise the sugar level well above my powers of digestion." "Sadly, for once, style and quality are not enough to keep the Umbrellas of Cherbourg from leaving damp puddles." "Indeed, the cast does more screen shifting than a pavilion atten-dant." "But all this piece of overblown whimsy did for me was to remind me never to get my car seen at a garage where people sing."

Well, that was that. We took the bad reviews in our stride and ran over to the other producer's home and production office. We wanted to know if we should close the show or try to keep it afloat. We waited a few days to see if word of mouth would pick up the box office receipts, but to no avail. I had to return to Los Angeles the next day so Roy was left to close the show at the end of the week.

It was raining when we all piled onto the train to Gatwick and I waved a teary goodbye to my husband. It was strangely reminiscent of the close of the first act of *Umbrellas*.

Roy had plans to go with Richard and his wife, Aida, that Sunday to Stonehenge, which they very much wanted to see. Two of our other friends, were going to join them. I felt sad that I couldn't go with them. Stonehenge is a place I've always felt spiritually drawn to. The family, however, was off to Los Angeles on Freddy Laker where we unhappily met up with the Rugby team. Apparently, they were not coming back in triumph either.

It was a long flight, but as soon as we landed, I made it out first to go through customs and to try to catch a through-flight to Palm Springs. I waved goodbye to my in-laws and ran through the airport carrying my luggage to catch my connecting flight.

I knew my kids would be at the airport with their smiling faces beaming from ear to ear. I really had missed them and couldn't wait to give them their little presents. I knew that it wouldn't matter to them if the show was successful or not. They just wanted to see Mommy and Daddy. Through children you really get in touch with what is important in life. You can have many failures and disappointments around you but they are miniscule compared to the love of your children.

I called Roy in London as soon as I got home but was unable to reach him for two days. I was worried, so I called the production office and was told that Roy would get back to me soon. He finally called and sounded quite strange and remote. Our friend Richard had died in my husband's arms at Stonehenge from a cerebral hemorrhage. I couldn't speak and Roy was sobbing on the phone. All I could say was that I was sorry. Then a wave of total despair and exhaustion came over me. It was such a long distance between us. I wanted to be close to him, right there beside him, to console him.

There was nothing either of us could say on the phone. I listened quietly and then finally hung up. I wanted to fly back to London immediately to be with Roy. The closing of the show meant nothing now. Values and priorities change. To be with the one that you love is most important.

It now seems strange to be looking back on these memories. I haven't forgotten Richard, our friends and family and the four-story mews. I can remember lots of cold water, a dumb waiter, opening night, the limousines, Scotland Yard, the Plexiglas panels and Stonehenge.

Aida, Richard's wife, who was quite ill on opening night, called a few months after his death to say that she was pregnant. She had conceived a few days before he died.

This was the nature of show business: A show opened; a show closed. For us, a friend was lost. I don't see this story as being a sad one. A unique and different one perhaps, but I do see it as a reassurance of life and love.

CHAPTER THIRTEEN

We Relocate to New England

Permanent in Portsmouth

I knew my friend, Ann Gratton, from Paris where we wrote a screenplay together. She lived in Portsmouth, New Hampshire. When we both returned from Europe we kept in touch, and Roy and I went to visit her and her family. She took us on a tour of her town, and we both fell in love with it.

There was the Theatre-by the Sea, a 265 seat, three-quarter thrust stage theater. There was the 900 seat Music Hall, soon to have a new owner. We decided right then that we wanted to move to the East Coast.

Theater by-the-Sea was not doing well and probably going bankrupt, while the Music Hall was being refurbished.

A light bulb went off. We decided we would produce *Peter Pan* there, with our friend Nehemiah Persoff as Captain Hook. I would play Mrs. Darling, and dance in the ensemble. I would also choreograph the show because I knew the original Jerome Robbins choreography.

This was in the winter of 1985 and by 1986, we sold our house in Los Angeles and bought a house in Rye, New Hampshire, six miles from Portsmouth. We would start a new life in New England

Roy at the time was conducting a tryout show in Washington DC, which was going to Broadway. I was working as an agent. We moved the whole family to Rye in September, 1986.

Shahna was an exchange student in Columbia, South America. Joshua was at Camp in Maine and Roy was in DC. What a job of coordination of moving and getting everyone together in our new home! I did it all myself. Thank me very much, family!

In September, school started and we were all together except for Roy who was in New York opening his show.

Our first venture in Portsmouth was to create a performing arts academy, which we called PAPA: The Portsmouth Academy of Performing Arts. We hadn't anticipated that the name would catch on because of its familial connotations, and the "mom and pop" nature of the enterprise when we started out.

We rented a three hundred square foot space in an old button factory, bought twenty folding chairs, and opened for business. We were both teaching classes. I worked primarily with kids, and Roy taught adults. We both had a little trouble adjusting to a place that was not very accepting to newcomers whose grandparents didn't land on Plymouth Rock with the first settlers. Welcome to New England!

We eventually abandoned our little guerilla theater and moved into the vacant Theatre by the Sea, which, before its untimely demise, had been a cultural beacon of the Seacoast. We renamed it the Seacoast Repertory Theatre. Owners Joe Sawtelle and Sumner Weinbaum gave us the key to the building and we renamed it the Seacoast Repertory Theatre.

A local newspaper article referred to Roy's career, and listed a number of my professional accomplishments, not the least of which was the Mouseketeers and Hollywood.

Instead of these being calling cards to a welcoming new community, the locals were very suspicious, saying "If you say you've done all those big show biz things, why are 'ya coming heya?" Worse still, was our dinner with the man who wrote the article, introducing us to the community. Sitting around the dinner table at our home, his wife said, "I've never eaten with Jews before."

We were a tough sell, to say the least, and it took many years of hard work and successful classes and shows to break down the barrier of being seen as carpetbaggers. "We're just going to have to put our heads down and push the rock up the hill," Roy said.

My classes were wonderful. The kids had never experienced anything like what I was teaching. I combined poetry, dance, music, monologues, commercials, and a little madness into their somewhat limited opportunities for self-expression. I started producing and staging more audience-friendly musicals starring both kids and adults. We did six original children's shows a year, in addition to our main shows.

It took us five years to take root, because there was so much distrust. It always reminded me of the scene from the movie "High Noon" where Gary Cooper walked alone down a deserted street to face the gang who came to take over the town, not a friend in sight.

While at Seacoast Rep, I began a new phase of my career: directing. I directed and choreographed *Bye Bye Birdie*, by Charles Strouse, *Ah Wilderness*, by Eugene O'Neill, *Our Town* by Thornton Wilder, *Brighton Beach Memoirs* by Neil Simon, *The Summer of '42: The Musical* and *Harold and Maude*. Together, Roy and I collaborated on nearly 300 shows that we mounted during our nearly 20 years.

While doing all of that, I cast TV movies and commercials all over New England. As the Theatre's casting director, with trips to New York several times a year, I had the advantage of my own history as a performer, which gave me the added insight, and empathy that only can be achieved by experience.

One of my proudest accomplishments in Portsmouth was the creation of "Senior Moments." We started with a group of twenty seniors, minimum age fifty-five. No maximum! The seniors wrote and performed their own plays and musicals, which we mounted. They were wonderfully received and became staples of each season. I'm glad that I finally succeeded in convincing Roy to give the program a try. From the first performance, with a ticket price of $5.00, I grew the program to multiple sell-out performances of each of the six shows we did every year.

We grew local talent, young and old. I started attending the New England Theatre Conferences each spring, where college students came to audition for summer stock jobs around New England.

The management of Seacoast Rep was truly an equal partnership. Roy and I supported each other in all areas, creative and business. That we didn't always agree was one of the secrets to our success. Roy's interactions with everyone were predicated on his nurturing personality and the fact that he never wanted to hurt anyone's feelings. I was the "black hat" to his "white." No euphemisms for me. Tell it like it is, and consequences be damned. Give me the bottom line! We were a good balance, and the quality of the shows reflected the success of our partnership.

Since we were not an Actor's Equity house, with a set pay scale and benefits, and since Seacoast Rep had gained a formidable reputation, we hired a lot of professional actors on Guest Artist Contracts, as recommended by Equity. But we never turned our back on gifted local performers.

The guy you went to school with, or the mom who drove the carpool, donned greasepaint, mounted the stage and performed alongside seasoned professionals. That was one of the keys to our acceptance and our success. We were a professional theatre for the community.

We were always pushing the envelope. We did *The Rocky Horror Show* every Halloween weekend. We did *Hedwig and the Angry Inch* before it went to Broadway. We worked with young people, teenagers, adults and senior citizens. We also did a production of one of Roy's musicals, *Minding the Store*. Bradley Dean, who went on to Broadway leading roles, played Herbert Marcus. Roy and I worked tirelessly to give back what we had been given so early in our careers: a professional work ethic, a nurturing and supportive environment and an opportunity to grow and flourish as performers.

We brought our beloved friend, Bonnie Franklin of *One Day at a Time*, to star in Shirley Valentine. Roy and Bonnie played opposite each other in their high school musical at Beverly Hills High. Her passing several years ago was a tremendous personal and professional loss. We invited Tony Award Winner John Rubinstein (*Children of a Lesser God*) and his wife to perform *Love Letters*.

We brought Lucy Arnaz to Portsmouth to play Maria Callas in *Master Class*. Her performance was the thing that legends are made of.

At the end of the play, a huge image of the audience at La Scala Opera House was projected across the entire stage behind Lucy. It was a miraculous *coup de theatre*. Roy and I went to the producer of the Broadway original and asked him where we could get the slide and projector. He put us in touch with the designer who invented the process, and he allowed us to use the original. At the end of our production, the

L-R: Maria Callas, Lucy and Roy.

audience reached under their seats to pick up roses we left there, and enthusiastically threw them up on stage at Lucy's feet. What a joyful moment and experience. Thank you, Lucy!

Neither sleet nor snow would keep us from presenting actors on a stage for a live audience. We never canceled a show. Even when a mighty blizzard dropped four feet of snow during the Christmas run of "Camelot." From the beginning of our careers in the wilds of Montana, even when there were never more than a handful of people in the audience, we decided that if there was only one person, there was an "audience!" The show always goes on. Seventy-five people tramped through the ice and snow to see the show.

The Rocky Horror Show was, by far, our most outrageous production, second only to *Hedwig and the Angry Inch.* Audience members dressed in costume. The male president of our board of directors shockingly showed up dressed in a teddy and mesh stockings.

On one particular Saturday midnight performance, I noticed two uniformed cops standing at the back of the auditorium. I thought they were going to close us

Music Man at Seacoast Rep.

down. I met them at the back of the house. "A neighbor called and told us to come here and shut you down." A policeman told me. "There is no legal reason why we have to shut you down. Do you mind if we stay and watch the show?"

We Add the Ogunquit Playhouse

The seventy-five-year-old Ogunquit Playhouse in Maine was a short 16-mile commute from Portsmouth. It was three times the size of Seacoast Rep. It was an Equity house and a national landmark.

Word about our *Master Class* traveled fast. Board members from the Ogunquit Playhouse came to the performance and shortly afterward asked Roy to take over as their Artistic Director. We decided that I would continue on at Seacoast while Roy brought the Ogunquit Playhouse back to life after a period of declining sales. After Ogunquit's ten-week season was over, Roy joined me back at our first love, the Seacoast Repertory Theatre.

After being in Rye for eight years, we moved to a house in Maine which was between both theaters.

For the last six years that we lived in Maine, Roy was running Ogunquit. In time, we started a Children's Theatre there, which proved to be a lifeline for Ogunquit's rebirth. I taught every Saturday and weekday afternoons. And we added *Senior Moments*, too.

I soon discovered that the stubborn New England mentality we met in Portsmouth was tame compared to Maine! We suggested purchasing a gazebo to sell liquor during intermission. "Nevah done that befowah." Any proposed change was a crisis.

There was a huge grass field on one side of the theatre and another huge grass field on the other side. The Playhouse was paying $10,000 per summer to rent one of the fields for parking. Roy went to the Board of Directors and asked them the name of the field's owner. "I'll go and negotiate with them and see if we can get a better deal." They told him it was non-negotiable. "I'll talk to the owners of the other field and see if we can get it for $5,000." Roy told them.

"We own that land!" they told Roy. He responded, "Why don't you park there instead of paying for the other one?"

Their reply: "We've nevah done thaaat befowah!"

CHAPTER FOURTEEN

Happy C-A-M-P-E-R-S

C-A-M-P Portsmouth

In 1986, Roy and I founded The Portsmouth Academy of Performing Arts Camp, which morphed into C-A-M-P: Creative-Arts-Music-Performance. This was a two-week summer camp with total emphasis on performance arts of all types.

The kids in our Children's Theatre spent busy days and weekends rehearsing and performing. Two weeks at an overnight camp with days and nights filled with music, dance and writing were a welcome respite from the "responsibilities" of being a student. Kids and teachers, counselors and directors worked to improve their performance skills. Their parents always confirmed that C-A-M-P improved all of their schoolwork and relationships!

C-A-M-P has been a life-changing experience for many. We started with kids ranging in age from seven through seventeen and an incredible staff of professional writers, composers, choreographers, directors and musical directors. Over the years, we watched the kids grow up and start careers. In time, a couple of my students returned to teach.

Campers traveled from near and far, but they came mostly from New York and New England.

Dance, voice and music were transforming and beautiful when the kids stimulated the creative parts of their brains. Some of the kids came, not because they had specific talents in voice or dance, but because they each had something to share: themselves. That was the most prized accomplishment: we provided the creative sandbox in which they could discover and develop their amazing individuality It was an amazing gift for us to watch these kids develop and grow their talents and then go on to Broadway auditions and successes.

We started with twenty-five campers and over the years, averaged about eighty campers. That was the limit we set for ourselves. It was important to us to be on a hands-on, first name basis with everyone.

I've always been a firm believer in mixing ages in every class because the younger ones have no inhibitions, while the older kids have already built walls around themselves. And the younger kids learn from the older kids because the teens are more polished. The concept works beautifully. Everyone works together during the day. But at night, the kids are housed by age and gender in their respective cabins. Most of our teachers graduated from musical theatre college programs or were already working professionals.

C-A-M-P is musical theatre heaven!

We sing in the mornings. All kinds of choral music. Everybody is together. Afternoons, we split into different electives: dance, acting, Shakespeare, poetry, writing monologues, voice, filmmaking and rock bands.

When the parents come back two weeks later to pick up their kids, we put on a very special talent show. Every single camper performed at what he or she did best. It could be the reading of a poem, the singing of a classic rock song, dancing to original choreography, or just standing up and saying, "Here I am. And I am perfect, just the way I am."

Each year we feature what is current on Broadway for that season. It was incredible to see our show in

2016: we did two songs from the Broadway smash musical "Hamilton." Everyone learned the rap and pulled it off without a hitch. I don't know who was more excited, the performers or the parents. It was unbelievable.

I always taught: "You always have to act as a team. You have to be together. You can't just be where you want to be. You are a link and everyone else depends on you." What a lesson. Young people are always up for the challenge. Even the counselors got into the act with their very own talent show and strutted their stuff to the delighted ridicule of their campers.

Each cabin contributed to their own original mini-musical. Each show contained three songs, dialogue and a dance routine, woven into the fabric of a tremendously entertaining show. Sometimes heartbreaking, often hysterical, and always highly personal, the shows became a megaphone for shouting out, "Here I am!"

There are many differently themed campfires. We always start with the Sufi Welcome. I pick a person and we stand face-to-face in front of the campfire. I use my hands and create a triangle and look directly into my partner's eyes through the triangle. And then they create the same triangle and both our eyes lock into an intense stare. Next, we take each other's hands, put them on each other's heart and feel each other's heartbeat. Then we reverse the process so that the other person is completely engaged. After experiencing the heartbeat, we look again into each other's eyes and fall into a heartfelt hug. The celebration of each camper spreads like a giant embrace among everyone. The kids continue inviting others into the Sufi Welcome until every camper has been a part of the gift of community.

Our second campfire is "S'more's Night." All the staff and counselors perform for the campers, giving the campers an incentive to start performing and create their own performances for each other in preparation for the final night.

Our final campfire on the last night of camp starts with a huge banquet in the dining hall. We present awards to everybody, campers and counselors and teachers. Funny awards focused on inside jokes. That's when I perform my infamous ballet from "Swan Lake." I flutter my arms and eyelashes as I literally sing Tchaikovsky's melody of the Dying Swan that accompanies the swan's death. I flutter across the stage. As the music reaches its climax, I begin to die, fluttering all the more fiercely. Finally, as I am bent over on my knee, gasping my last Swan's breath, Roy pantomimes holding a rifle, and shouts "Bang!" at the top of his lungs and shoots me dead and I fall over like a tree, to the uproarious laughter of the whole camp!

After dinner on the final night, we form a circle outside in the grove and each camper receives a candle. The head counselor, or Guru-in-Residence, Roy, lights the first candle and the flame is passed around the circle, one camper at a time. We then take a long walk to the campfire site. We all sit down and many empty their hearts of what is most important to them at that precious time in their lives. With lighted candles in our hands, we stand around the campfire. Roy and I share our thoughts, make a silent prayer and join our candles with the campfire. Everyone follows and the smoke from everyone's dreams rises to the stars.

When we joined in that moment of sharing. I thought I'd never be able to surrender that blessed experience and leave it behind after thirty years. But I did. Not without some sadness, but with celebration too. Celebration for a job well done, of bringing people of all ages together, of leading them into themselves, finding their voices and then inviting them out to share what they've learned and who they became.

"Time flies when you're having fun," the old adage says. Hard to believe I'm 76 and Roy is 77 at this writing. Our last year at C-A-M-P, we rode around in an electric golf cart. Not because we couldn't walk (thankfully), but because we wanted to take it all in. We wanted a lasting picture of 30 years of commitment and caring, celebrating and singing about the joys of being young, gifted and facing a limitless future.

The postscript of our lifelong adventure in the arts was creating The Musical Theatre Works of Santa Fe, where we moved to in 2006. We began to replicate our success in Portsmouth. We taught classes, produced shows and relished the interaction with young and emerging talent.

We created Camp Santa Fe, modeled after our wonderful camp experiences in New England. We even mounted a Musical Theatre Festival to encourage new writers for the musical theatre to submit their work for consideration to produce their shows in workshop.

This was a direct outgrowth of Roy's increasing dedication to his own writing. He has written five musicals, three of which have had successful regional productions. He and I felt it was time to begin nurturing ourselves and each other: Roy writing shows, and I writing this memoir.

Musical Theater Works

Our latest project is Musical Theater Works, offering students a comprehensive education and training in the performing arts. Musical Theater Works is all about show business. The class list covers the ABC's of performance: Musical Theater, Dance, Voice, Private Vocal and Instrumental Instruction.

Rehearsal of *Les Miz* at the Greer Garson Theatre, in Santa Fe, NM.

The school curriculum is drawn from the vast wealth of experience and success we've had in the performing arts. We've lived in the limelight, center stage, on television, recordings, film, Broadway theaters and symphonic stages, creating images and music that endure. Our Student alumni have performed on Broadway stages and boast film credits.

Working side-by-side, we have coached and inspired new generations of musicians, performers, writers and technicians, ensuring the melody will linger on and on.

Musical Theatre Works productions are performed by children and adults, backed by a full orchestra. We've done the Broadway classics: *Annie*, *Les Miz*, and *Fiddler on the Roof*, as well as original Santa Fe debut performances of *Adolessons, Carol of Christmas* and *Sycamore Street Kite Flying Club*, which had a workshop at Lincoln Center in New York City. Per Roy, "our students discover their own perfection!"

Our collaboration continues and was expanded with the presentation of two Santa Fe Musical Theatre Festivals.

Here is the 2014 press release for the first festival:

> The Santa Fe Musical Theatre Festival brings Composers, Lyricists, and Librettists from all over the world to prepare and present original works for invited industry professionals and the general public. Authors will be mentored by Guest Artists from the professional world of Musical Theatre, who will come to Santa Fe to work with the artists and help to shepherd their shows to the next level.

> Solicitation of new works will be from major University and Conservatory programs. In addition, Professional colleagues, Regional Theatres, and Independent producers will be encouraged to recommend works, each of which will be reviewed by a select review committee. Unsolicited material will be reviewed after professional submissions have been adjudicated.

A second Musical Theatre Festival was presented in 2015 at the Lensic Performing Arts Center of Santa Fe.

We were in our early forties when we started in Portsmouth. It seemed only a heartbeat away and then, all of a sudden, we were in our sixties in Portsmouth and seventies in Santa Fe!

Our kids were grown up and had moved on, establishing two very successful careers, Josh as the Technical Director and Producer for NPR Music and Shahna is the Head of Psychiatry at the Palo Alto Medical Foundation.

It seemed as if we had been working 24-hour days for nearly forty years. We were both exhausted. Intuitively, we both felt it was time to create a different lifestyle. We found out that we couldn't even pronounce the word "retirement!"

Onward!

CHAPTER FIFTEEN

The Teacher Becomes the Student

The first time I began teaching was at the Beverly Hills Academy of Music, founded by Olga Melchione, who took me under her wing. I was fifteen, and she expanded my horizons beyond performing, to include teaching and working with young people, which I loved from the start. I taught stretching exercises to introduce the students to the mechanics of the body and how they could control them.

One day, a young mother arrived with a group of her children and neighbors. They were the most rambunctious group of kids I had ever encountered. The mother wanted them to channel their energies into movement and dance. What they really needed was a corral and some kid-police!

I started with isolation exercises and control moves, focusing on very specific parts of the body: eyes, neck, and knees. This helps the student feel comfortable and to relax and focus. Except that not a single kid could focus. And my focus was split amongst all of them. I never saw that mom, or those kids, again.

My take away was that less is more when it came to the number of students concerned. I was discouraged for quite some time. Eventually, I reached a comfort zone working with small groups of young kids. I learned that smaller classes are much more effective.

My professional teaching career began at the Community Center in Palm Springs in the early 1980s. The director hired me to teach acting to young kids and I began my first Babes on Stage Class teaching songs from *Peter Pan* and *Sesame Street*, along with songs Roy had written especially for the class. This class was to prove a hallmark of my teaching for years to come.

Teaching Acting

I also created the Young Actors Lab, in which I started off with poetry and Shakespeare, taught scene work, singing, movement and dancing. I was totally involved, and focused. To my great pleasure, the children reflected my enthusiasm and commitment. They were like little sponges, so open to everything I taught. They were all equal in my eyes and, therefore, in theirs. Age differences didn't matter. What mattered was that we all participated fully, in accordance with our unique abilities. The concept of competition was never introduced. We treated all ages the same, and taught everybody as adults.

I am totally focused on my students during classes. Making sure they continue to get better. I am a teacher, mentor and collaborator, inspiring kids to get more out of themselves.

Everyone brings his/her strengths and weaknesses to the forefront. My job is to accentuate the former and strengthen the latter. I have always believed that the students who work the hardest last the longest. They are more committed and more passionate. To culminate all the classroom study and workshops, the students perform in recitals and special shows throughout the year.

I have mantras for training young people:

FOCUS- always keep your eye on the target.

LISTEN- it's not about what you are saying, it's about what the other person is saying.

PRACTICE- do it again- but better. And, better and... you get the idea!

MEMORIZATION- learn by content, not just by rote. Learn not only your lines, or the other person's lines, but where do you come from? And where do you go? And most importantly, "Why?" What does it all mean?

AND FOCUS- AGAIN!

AUTHENTICITY is also a major part of the process. Finding the truth in yourself about a character or situation. Not "acting" it. Believing it. And transmitting it to others.

The cardinal rule in my classes is never be afraid to make a fool of yourself. Truth can be found in excess, but never in fear! You have to find yourself in each character that you play. You can't just play at being a character. You really have to discover that character deep within yourself.

Sometimes the actors turn into the people they are playing and get so involved that they lose themselves, and, thereby, lose control. But the actor must always be in charge. It is his/her job to fill the production with his essence, and to tell the audience exactly what he/she expects of them. And sometimes the hardest roles have very few lines.

I encourage the kids to empty their minds before performing. Get rid of all the people talking around you. Noises! Thoughts! When your mind is empty, it is easy to absorb everything around you.

Another basic: Please yourself! You don't have to please everybody, but you have to be true to yourself.

As a teacher I've also learned that giving kids responsibilities helps them grow and succeed.

I continually tell my students: "You have to be disciplined. Work hard and continue your growth. Always be at the top of your game."

Then there's that continuous fear of failing that surfaces in all the kids. Fear of not being wanted! Or having the wrong hair-color or the wrong look. Whatever the reason: fear of being rejected.

I've discovered that my role as a teacher is constantly changing. Sometimes I am an equal with the students and sometimes I am way ahead in my thinking and actions. When I am teaching, I am also learning at the same time. The kids teach me. I become the student. The end result is that we all grow and learn from each other, so go out into the world and travel and discover who you really are.

Teaching Dance

There is something more to a dancer than the physical movement of dancing. I am a dancer, and dancing exists in my whole body. Music is the source. Its rhythms, its sounds, its silence all determine the shape of a dance. Dance requires my ultimate commitment, both physical and mental. It is all consuming, and that's why I love it.

Listed below are my DANCE ESSENTIALS and definitions:

In the beginning, there is the BREATH: it is what connects your inner self to the physical world.

RHYTHM: If you ain't got the rhythm, you ain't got it.

TIMING: In music, timing is the division and accentuation of different beats. In dance, timing is the tool with which to learn the steps and execute the choreography. In comedy, timing determines the effectiveness of the humor; in dance, the timing is the structure on which the movement is shaped.

STAMINA: Strength and endurance. A dancer feels the music throughout the body. A dancer feels the music coming out of the pores to the point that it can been seen. Dancing is all or nothing. There is no room for pretense: a smile must come from within. The expression of face and body must reflect all of life's experience until that moment. Authenticity is unmistakable, as is deceit.

GRACE: A dancer has a gracious flow throughout the entire body. It's more than just the sense of smoothness and control. Grace is the spiritual and physical involvement that lifts the merely "good" to the very great, by causing the heart of the audience to join with yours, beating as one.

MEMORIZATION: Dance classes train dancers to memorize their steps by audible counts. In time, the memorization process becomes automatic. Hand movements. Body movements. Facial expressions. The way you hold your head, arms and legs. It's very important to learn how to hold yourself.

Dance is a process. Dancers are always in class when they are not performing. The body demands it, the mind relishes it and the spirit depends on it.

So, what is the essence of being a dancer? Energy. Movement. Commitment. Purpose. Focus. Discipline. Preparation. Honesty. And hard work! Having talent, in and of itself, is not sufficient. To paraphrase an old saying, "Dance is ten percent inspiration and ninety percent perspiration." Stages, ballet schools and concert halls are littered with dreams of dancers who thought that having talent was enough. Only practice, practice and more practice make a dancer.

My favorite Shakespeare passage has been a vital part of my teaching repertoire since day one. "The Seven Ages of Man" from *As You Like It* is universal, expressive and a true classic. It beautifully sums up the nature of birth and death, as well as the stages of life, so relevant to the theatre.

> All the world's a stage,
> And the men and women merely players,
> They have their exits and entrances,
> And one man in his time plays many parts,
> His acts being seven ages. At first the infant,
> Mewling and puking in the nurse's arms.
> Then, the whining schoolboy with his satchel
> And shining morning face, creeping like a snail
> Unwillingly to school. And then the lover,
> Sighing like a furnace, with a woeful ballad
> Made to his mistress' eyebrow. Then a soldier,
> Full of strange oaths, and bearded like the pard,
> Jealous in honour, sudden, and quick in quarrel,
> Seeking the bubble reputation
> Even in the cannon's mouth. And then the justice
> In fair round belly, with good capon lin'd,
> With eyes severe and beard of formal cut,
> Full of wise saws, and modern instances,
> And so he plays his part. The sixth age shifts
> Into the lean and slipper'd pantaloons,
> With spectacles on nose, and pouch on side,
> His youthful hose well sav'd, a world too wide
> For his shrunk shank, and his big manly voice,
> Turning again towards childish treble, pipes
> And whistles in his sound. Last scene of all,
> That ends this strange eventful history,
> Is second childishness and mere oblivion,
> Sans teeth, sans eyes, sans taste, sans everything.

Dedication: To All Students of Performing Arts

If you haven't guessed by now, this book is for all the prospective young performers contemplating a career in the arts. Bravo, and my love and best wishes to you all!!

Throughout my teaching career, I've had the privilege of working with many extraordinarily gifted young performers. From the Seacoast Repertory Theatre in Portsmouth, New Hampshire to the Ogunquit Playhouse in Maine, each venue developed into a fertile laboratory for young talent.

As a proud teacher, I feel compelled to list some of my outstanding performers. These are but a few. All of them are talented, and I am sure there are more like them reading these very lines right now.

At Seacoast Rep, Sebastian Arcelus starred in *I Love You, You're Perfect, Now Change* and *Big River*. Sebastian made his Broadway debut in *Rent* and starred as Bob Gaudio in the Broadway production of *Jersey Boys*. He also appeared in the TV series *Madam Secretary* and *House of Cards*.

At 13, Phoenix Avalon brought his 'fiddle' to life on stage in Musical Theatre Works production of *Fiddler on the Roof*. He has soloed with Performance Santa Fe, The New Mexico Philharmonic and the Boulder Symphony. Phoenix was awarded a full scholarship to Julliard.

Alison Cusano performed in many musicals at Seacoast Repertory, including *The Summer of '42* which I directed. She starred in the Broadway run of *One Night with Janis Joplin*.

Bradley Dean starred in the Seacoast Rep's production of the Neiman Marcus musical *Minding the Store*. He later starred in the Broadway revival of *A Little Night Music* and played Sir Galahad in the musical comedy *Spamalot* on Broadway.

A 12-year-old Matthew Gillmore took his first dance steps at CAMP in Maine. He graduated from Julliard and is now in a professional dance company. He has performed the works of the great choreographers Merce Cunningham, Jerome Robbins and many more. He is the recipient of the Grace Kelly Award for Ballet.

After starting at Seacoast Rep at 12, Bryan Knowlton went on to receive the Helen Hayes Award in 2014 for Outstanding Lead Actor in *A Chorus Line*. He has become an active director/ choreographer throughout the United States with shows such as *Mama Mia*, *Saturday Night Fever*, and *The Hunchback of Notre Dame*.

Stephen Lucas made his theatrical debut at age 6, playing the son of Anna in *The King and I* at Seacoast. He was a standby for Elder Price in *The Book of Mormon* and went on to play the role on the national tour.

Starting as the youngest boy in *Fiddler on the Roof* at Seacoast, Tim Shea developed into a versatile tenor who has appeared in the national tours of *Rock of Ages* and Andrew Lloyd Webber's *School of Rock*.

Amy Spanger played leading roles at Seacoast Rep launching a career which led to the first national touring of company of *Rent* and a Tony nomination for her role of Bianca in *Kiss Me Kate*.

At age 12, Sarah Styles starred in the title role in *Annie* at Seacoast Rep. She was a Tony nominee for best featured actress in *Hand to God* on Broadway. She played one of the leads in *Tootsie* on Broadway.

Stephen Tewksbury was Tony in West Side Story at Seacoast Rep. and went on to a Broadway career, which includes *Kinky Boots*, *Phantom of the Opera*, *Miss Saigon*, and *Beauty and the Beast*.

Josh Young made his debut at Seacoast Rep in *Titanic* as well as appearing in other productions. He played the role of Judas in the Broadway revival of *Jesus Christ Superstar* for which he was nominated for the Tony Award for Best Featured Actor in a Musical.

Afterword

I don't think I fully matured until this past year! Can you imagine over fifty years of marriage, and not quite mature yet? I knew I was a late bloomer, but I didn't know how late!

Walking the beaches in Todo Santos, Baja Sur, Mexico with Roy everyday almost puts me into some sort of trance. Dharma! Going to Dharma lectures every Sunday with Dr. Robert Hall (since deceased) made me realize that forgiving the past is the only way to move on with life. That forgiving the past made me free. Forgiving the past enabled me to face reality.

Earliest memories of my young life are all about music and dance. I am grateful my mother encouraged me to practice piano every day.

Dancing with Balanchine. Dancing with the Mouseketeers and in the movies and, most of all, dancing on stage created vibrant passions in my life.

Roy told me that every time I came back from teaching a class, I was a brighter and happier person.

Dancing and hearing the music and hearing Roy composing...music was, and is, my underlying heartbeat.

I also realized that learning is a continuous process. Life is a continuous process. And I think that's what keeps us going.

Celebrating all the things I've done and passing those lessons and accomplishments on to my beloved children is an affirmation of my life's work.

Afterword?

Perhaps "FOREWORD" is a better way to end this book....

I danced. I sang. I cried and laughed. I triumphed and failed, and tried again. I love and am deeply loved by Roy. I am blessed with two extraordinary children, Shahna and Joshua, my son-in-law Jeremy and my grandson, Jonah. I watched my students win awards and establish successful careers on and off Broadway, in films and on television. I have seen others live their passions. And I have lived mine. I am still living mine with new experiences...new art, new museums, new theatre- new countries, new people, new acquaintances. I could go on; I encourage you to do the same...

And I have roared. Finally, I have become

The Mouseketeer that ROARED!

Acknowledgments

Special thanks to Linda Krull, of Santa Fe, New Mexico, an amazing friend and confidant who encouraged and supported my efforts in creating this memoir from the very beginning.

My husband Roy and our children Shahna and Joshua Who support me through their bountiful faith and love.

Wendy Rains, first editor and cheerleader in the singing of the Mouseketeer theme song at a luncheon she arranged in Todos Santos, Baja, where I realized the universal and lasting importance of the show in so many lives.

Randall Nakashima from the originalmmc.com website, friend to all Mousekeeters who rediscovered many of the original shows and put the pieces together so that they could be enjoyed by all.

Diane Pershing for her insights and recollections.

Tony and Judy Richman (Original Mouseketeer) for their lifelong support.

Joyce and Steve Weinberg for friendship from the beginning.

Ann Gratton Zeller with whom I began writing in Paris.

Drs. Lonnie and Paul Zeltzer for their encouragement for me to believe in myself.

Judith and Michael McGiveney

Robin and DD Frontiere

Joel and Deborah Rogosin

And all those gifted artists whose paths and careers I may have influenced as a director, writer, choreographer, and teacher. And to all those whose talents and humanity have contributed to my professional life and my growth as a fellow artist.

Colophon

This volume of *The Mouseketeer That Roared* was compiled through a series of taped interviews with Eileen Rogosin. Interviews were transcribed and edited by Linda Krull. Combined with compositions that Eileen wrote throughout her life.

About Theme Park Press

Theme Park Press publishes books primarily about the Disney company, its history, culture, films, animation, and theme parks, as well as theme parks in general.

Our authors include noted historians, animators, Imagineers, and experts in the theme park industry.

We also publish many books by first-time authors, with topics ranging from fiction to theme park guides.

And we're always looking for new talent. If you'd like to write for us, or if you're interested in the many other titles in our catalog, please visit:

www.ThemeParkPress.com

• •

Theme Park Press Newsletter

Subscribe to our free email newsletter and enjoy:

- ♦ Free book downloads and giveaways
- ♦ Access to excerpts from our many books
- ♦ Announcements of forthcoming releases
- ♦ Exclusive additional content and chapters
- ♦ And more good stuff available nowhere else

To subscribe, visit www.ThemeParkPress.com, or send email to newsletter@themeparkpress.com.

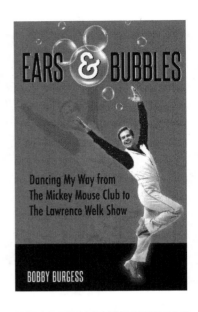
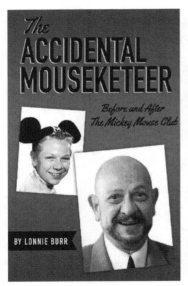

Made in the USA
San Bernardino, CA
01 July 2020